THE CINEMA OF
JOHN FORD
BY JOHN BAXTER

The Cinema of JOHN FORD

A vital new study of Ford's filmic language and philosophy, in which John Baxter discusses a wide selection of this great director's films

In the same series,
produced by THE TANTIVY PRESS
and edited by Peter Cowie:

The Cinema of Orson Welles
by Peter Cowie
Hitchcock's Films
by Robin Wood
The Marx Brothers: Their World of
Comedy
by Allen Eyles
French Cinema Since 1946
(Vol. 1: *The Great Tradition*)
(Vol. 2: *The Personal Style*)
by Roy Armes
The Musical Film
by Douglas McVay
Buster Keaton
by J-P. Lebel
Animation in the Cinema
by Ralph Stephenson
Horror in the Cinema
by Ivan Butler
The Cinema of Joseph Losey
by James Leahy
Suspense in the Cinema
by Gordon Gow
The Cinema of Alain Resnais
by Roy Armes
A Dictionary of the Cinema
by Peter Graham
4 Great Comedians: Chaplin, Lloyd,
Keaton, Langdon
by Donald W. McCaffrey
Early American Cinema
by Anthony Slide
Griffith and the Rise of Hollywood
by Paul O'Dell

Hollywood in the Twenties
by David Robinson
Hollywood in the Thirties
by John Baxter
Hollywood in the Forties
by C. Higham and J. Greenberg
Hollywood in the Fifties
by Gordon Gow
Hollywood Today
by Pat Billings and Allen Eyles
British Cinema
by Denis Gifford
Religion in the Cinema
by Ivan Butler
The Cinema of Fritz Lang
by Paul M. Jensen
The Cinema of John Frankenheimer
by Gerald Pratley
The Cinema of François Truffaut
by Graham Petrie
Science Fiction in the Cinema
by John Baxter
The Cinema of Roman Polanski
by Ivan Butler
The Cinema of Josef von Sternberg
by John Baxter
The Cinema of Carl Dreyer
by Tom Milne
The Cinema of Otto Preminger
by Gerald Pratley
Ustinov in Focus
by Tony Thomas

The Cinema of

JOHN FORD

by
John Baxter

The International Film Guide Series

A. ZWEMMER
LONDON

A. S. BARNES & CO.
NEW YORK

Acknowledgements

I particularly want to thank Jeremy Boulton of the National Film Archive, London, who arranged so many screenings for me, and M. Jacques Ledoux, through whose courtesy the facilities of the Cinémathèque Royale de Belgique, Brussels, were made available. Thanks are also due to the Stills Archive and the Information Section of the British Film Institute, to the British Museum and the United States Collection staff of London University Library, as well as Doreen Lucas, Phil Hardy, and Allen Eyles of *Focus on Film* magazine. The stills used in this book are from films distributed by the following Companies—Columbia, M-G-M, Republic, 20th Century-Fox, RKO, Universal, Warner Brothers, and Paramount.

John Baxter

Cover design by Stefan Dreja, featuring
Ford with John Wayne

FIRST PUBLISHED 1971
Copyright © 1971 by John Baxter
Library of Congress Catalog Card No. 79–175640
SBN 302-02190-6 (U.K.)
SBN 0-498-01068-6 (U.S.A.)
Filmset by Keyspools Ltd, Golborne, Lancs.
Printed by C. Tinling and Co. Ltd, London and Prescot

PRINTED IN ENGLAND

Contents

"The United States themselves are essentially the greatest poem. Here at last is something in the doings of man that corresponds with the broadcast doings of day and night . . . Here is the hospitality which forever indicates heroes . . . Other states indicate themselves in their deputies, but the genius of the United States is not best or most in its executives or legislatures, not in its ambassadors or authors or colleges or churches or parlors, nor even in its newspapers or inventors . . . but always most in the common people. Their manners speech dress friendships—the freshness and candor of their physiognomy—the picturesque looseness of their carriage . . . their deathless attachment to freedom—their aversion to anything indecorous or soft or mean—the practical acknowledgement of the citizens of one state by the citizens of other states—the fierceness of their roused resentment—their curiosity and welcome of novelty—their self-esteem and wonderful sympathy—their susceptibility to a slight— the air they have of persons who never knew how it felt to stand in the presence of superiors—the fluency of their speech—their delight in music, the sure symptom of manly tenderness and native elegance of soul . . . their good temper and open-handedness—the terrible significance of their elections—the President's taking off his hat to them not they to him— these too are unrhymed poetry. It awaits the gigantic and generous treatment worthy of them."

Introduction, Leaves of Grass
WALT WHITMAN

1. The Last Missionary

By any standard, John Ford is one of the greatest directors the cinema has produced. His films, in their force, popular appeal and exploitation of the medium's resources are outstanding popular art, while their intricate moral structure and insight into the relationship of man and environment make them central to any understanding of American ideals. Few directors have proved themselves greater masters of, yet shown such shrewd disregard for the rules of the entertainment film. After an early career in that most rigid of disciplines, the Western, Ford essayed the gangster film, the documentary and the epic, respecting the rules of each but marking every film as the work of an individual talent. All these films are, of their kind, memorable, but they share a common viewpoint and attitude to character unique to Ford. Although his durability—one hundred and twelve features and many shorter films since 1917—alone would have warranted respect, it is his ability to adapt any subject as a vehicle for his philosophy that has made Ford a major figure in the cinema and inspired the admiration of artists as remote from his world as Ingmar Bergman and Jean-Luc Godard. Film-makers and critics politically and emotionally opposed to Ford's often simplistic and reactionary views unite in admiration of his genius in expressing them; on the level of invention at which he works, ideology is irrelevant.

But the ability to recognise Ford's genius does not necessarily lead to an understanding of it, or of the man behind the films. Since his critical "arrival" in 1934 with *The Informer*—his commercial success, even before the popular *The Iron Horse* in 1924, has been constant— succeeding generations of critics, while certain of Ford's skill and eminence, have seldom agreed on reasons for his appeal. The

Opposite : Ford with Hoot Gibson on location for THE HORSE SOLDIERS

"realism" praised in *The Informer* on its release bears little relationship to the realism for which *The Grapes of Wrath* was honoured five years later, while modern audiences find both films equally mannered and unreal by comparison with the spare accuracy of *The Searchers*. Yet by any standards of realism—historical accuracy, fidelity to agreed rules of human behaviour, rejection of irrelevant theatrical devices—none of them deserves the adjective "realistic". Clearly, realism is not what was meant, but critics have failed for forty years to produce a more accurate description of the quality common to these undoubtedly related and admirable films. We will continue to fail as long as we attempt to fit Ford's work to existing categories, and do not acknowledge that it supersedes even the forms in which he chooses to express himself. Elements of the archetypal Ford film come quickly to mind—Monument Valley, John Wayne, the Seventh Cavalry, a dance, a funeral, a fight—but only a fraction of Ford's films, not always the best, contain all these, and the effectiveness with which he uses them varies widely, as do the situations in which they are contained. A third of Ford's films are set outside the United States, and many others in American locales with little relationship to the highly individual landscape of *She Wore a Yellow Ribbon* and *Stagecoach*. Emphasis on the thematic consistency of a few Ford films had led to a categorisation that extends even to Ford himself, now thoroughly labelled as a direct and sentimental stylist with a *penchant* for outdoor Americana.

Yet it is dramatic proof of Ford's stature as an artist that no pigeon-hole has yet been found that will hold him for long. To analyse the Ford style, the Ford philosophy, the quintessential Ford hero is largely a matter of removing the partitions that he and his admirers have set up throughout his work; he must be defined by negatives. Ford is not primarily sentimental, simple, an action director, nor especially American; his interest in character and morality dictates his choice of plots and locales more than any nationalistic beliefs. If he is American, it is as Welles is American, in temperament. He is not an uncomplicated story-teller; suppression of narrative is part of his style, since it accentuates the flow of daily events and emphasises history at the expense of individual life. Nor does he faithfully record history; his versions of characters from Mary Queen of Scots through Abraham Lincoln to Douglas Mac-Arthur do not survive even the most passing critical examination as accurate portraits; they were not intended to. Ford's respect for landscape seems obvious, but a marked preference for theatrical and atypical areas like Yellowstone and Monument Valley, as well as his careful staging of exteriors and frequent indoor shooting of outdoor shots to gain specific effects, show that his use of nature is precise and symbolic.

The image of himself as a commercial director, catering to public taste and wishing only to entertain, is one Ford is at pains to support, but evidence of his popularity is meagre. Few of his films have made large profits, while critical acceptance is usually lamentably slow; except for productions like *Stagecoach* and *The Grapes of Wrath* most of Ford's films were treated disparagingly by critics and public on their release, and Ford criticism is a constant process of reassessment and upwards revaluation. His characters, it is often said, are realistic and warmly human, but since all his work embodies a strong moral lesson in the exposition of which each person has a precise function, people are more often types than individuals. Individuality, in fact, is a trait Ford finds an occasionally convenient but reprehensible deviation (hence his dislike of competitions and races, of which his films are almost totally bereft) but equally alien to him is the concept of equality. We live, Ford suggests, in a stratified moral and social structure, exercising rightful control over those below and owing a respect to those above that becomes adoration in the case of the truly great. Though concerned with mankind, Ford has little respect for the individual will, or for society except as an expression of historical order. The moral rules of his films allow no infringement by any person or group without the direst results.

With this in mind, the subject of tradition, often nominated as Ford's deepest concern, is seen in a new light. Tradition—"opinion

Ford, John Wayne, Ken Curtis, Maureen O'Hara, Chuck Roberson and Chuck Mayward on the set for WINGS OF EAGLES

or belief or custom handed down from ancestors to posterity" to quote the Concise Oxford definition—implies an uncritical acceptance of values whose guarantee is their age, but his characters have no respect for such ephemera. To Ford, moral truths are self-evident, formulated often in a vacuum, and occasionally in defiance of opinion handed down, *cf.* Tom Joad's rejection of parental authority in *The Grapes of Wrath* and a similar action by the Morgan sons in *How Green Was My Valley*. A reverence for tradition in the abstract, societal nostalgia, is a uniquely American concept, and its attachment to such varying aspects of Ford's work as a love of ritual and respect for the great dead is based on the assumption that America and its ideals dominate Fordian cinema. Ford no doubt loves his adopted country, but he is, after all, Irish by parentage, Catholic by faith and education, and a military aristocrat by inclination. None of these persuasions demand, even condone an adherence to tradition, but rather a respect for force that has as its justification self-evident moral right. Ford's soldiers do not obey orders because it is a tradition, but because it is their clear duty to do so, just as his pioneers do not dance merely because it is amusing; a dance, like a funeral or a fight, is a chance to affirm the principles of shared effort by which their community survives.

FORD AND CRITICISM

Most assumptions about Ford stem from a tendency to see his films almost completely in terms of plots and settings. While Howard Hawks's work is now often considered in the light of his insight into human relationships and Hitchcock with regard to the themes of guilt and redemption, Ford remains stranded in the horse-and-buggy criticism of the Forties, which chose to judge films in terms of story and social significance rather than underlying patterns of thought or action. The championship of Ford by the magazine *Sequence* in 1949–1951 and the enthusiastic essays in that magazine, mainly by Lindsay Anderson, that did much to revive waning interest in Ford's films, also set a critical tone that has survived to the Seventies, often to Ford's detriment. At the cost of establishing him as a major figure of the cinema, *Sequence* doomed Ford to be judged almost entirely in terms of his interest in and affection for American rural life and for the West, his respect for discipline and tradition, in short, for the superficial themes of his work rather than the films themselves. That much of Ford's best work is not American in setting nor simple and affectionate in style were facts rejected by the wholesale dismissal of more than half his work in Anderson's dictum that "the films which . . . one would select as Ford's most successful are all distinctively American in theme", as narrow an interpretation of the director's work as one could hope to find. Ford's long involvement with the scenarist Dudley Nichols, responsible for some of his most serious work, was rejected as a mistake, inconvenient productions like *The Fugitive* accused of a "sickly dishonesty" and, despite the director's own admiration of them, written off.

This mis-reading of Ford's work was all the more tragic for the skill, force and obvious affection for Ford as artist and man with which it was expressed. *Sequence's* intention, faced with the corruption of postwar Hollywood, to assert the craftsmanship and moral involvement of new European directors demanded, besides admiration for Fauvists like Dmytryk and Dassin, an ideal from the classic American cinema whose work could be offered as a model to Hollywood, and the magazine's editors elevated to this position a paragon Ford based on an illusory personality inferred from his available work. The basis of their selectivity is implicit in Anderson's summary of Ford's appeal; "unsophisticated and direct," he wrote, "his work can be enjoyed by anyone, regardless of cultural level, who has retained his sensitivity and subscribes to values primarily humane." Further articles about and interviews with Ford in *Sequence* and other magazines underlined this Lincolnian image. He was Honest John Ford, a reticent New England primitive, "the quiet man." Such a John Ford did not exist, has never existed, but it is regrettable, if understandable, that critics of the time, seldom able to view Ford's films in quantity, adopted the *Sequence* line without question. In the end, the judgement was one with which even Ford became bored. Of the production of *Seven Women,* a friend said, "Jack resents the fact that most people think of him as a director of cowboy pictures. He has decided to remind them of his versatility."

A certain contempt for theme is, in fact, implicit in Ford's approach to all his films, which is to accept an assignment and then, by skilful manipulation of his actors, a language of unscripted gestures and actions to make it a vehicle for his highly personal views.

Opposite : John Ford discusses a scene with Gloria Stewart on the set of AIR MAIL

No one sentence can sum up the complex mixture of philosophy, religious conviction, military custom, amateur sociology, Irish humour and respect for authority that is at the centre of Ford's vision of the world, but like the poems of Walt Whitman, an artist with whom Ford has a great deal in common, his films assert the essential rules of civilisation and society, in Whitman's words "the entire faith and acceptance of life which is the foundation of moral America." Ford and Whitman are concerned to celebrate rather than merely record, to praise their society, deify its great men and the morality that sustains them. Both respect natural nobility, discipline and order, and hope, in emphasising these virtues, to influence those to whom they speak. Ford, like Whitman, finds the strongest proof of man's instinctive desire for an orderly and moral existence in the history of the United States, but unlike the poet, who retreated into a more personal code of behaviour when events cast doubt on this belief, Ford manufactured for his films a fictitious America in which landscape, culture and society reflect his ideals. This nation, if it ever existed, died in the Civil War, but Ford continues, by example, parable and precept, to dramatise its values and ask us to emulate them. The beliefs and his statement of them stand immovably in the landscape of the cinema, as unyielding, as unavoidable and as historically irrelevant as the buttes of Monument Valley.

FORD AND HISTORY

In essence, Ford's subject is history, but history seen in the oblique and deceptive illumination of hind-sight and self-interest. More concerned to find a lesson in the past than to record it with any accuracy, Ford adapts incidents to his purpose with little regard for the reality of characters and events. His devotion to the song "Dixie" transcends the fact that it was not written in time for Lincoln to have admired it in *Young Mr. Lincoln,* and his view of the cavalry and the Civil War is his own to an extent that must surprise anybody who knows even a little of the truth. Frank Nugent, writer on many of

Ford, probably taken on location for THE HURRICANE

Ford's films, said he prepared for his work on *Fort Apache* and *She
Wore a Yellow Ribbon* by "reading every book on the Southwest I
could lay my weary eyes on. (Ford) sent me hotfooting to Tombstone
and Apache Pass and Cochise's Stronghold and to the pathetic little
markers showing where men had been spreadeagled and submitted to
the small Apache torture fires. After seven weeks of this I returned
to Hollywood full of erudition, steeped in Indian lore and cavalry
commands. 'You're satisfied with yourself?' Ford asked. I assured
him I was. 'Fine,' he said . . . 'Now forget everything you've read and
we'll start writing a movie about the cavalry.'" This disparity
between reality and legend is strongly featured in *Fort Apache* and

17

The Man Who Shot Liberty Valance, Ford suggesting in both cases that legend must have ascendancy over the truth if society is to benefit from a sacrifice. This is more than a Fordian quirk; he is stating what he feels to be a vital rule of society, that many men exist first as an example to others, the embodiment of a moral lesson, and only incidentally as individuals. One sees this more clearly in his treatment of leaders like Lincoln and MacArthur, his portraits of whom are glowing paragons, not real men. Lincoln's gawkiness, ugliness, and squeaky voice (on which even his great admirer Whitman commented), "the small-town lawyer, the crude small-time politician, State character, but comparative failure at forty" of Stephen Vincent Benet's description has disappeared; gone is MacArthur's ruthlessness and aristocratic contempt for the common soldier, and the vanity of Mary Queen of Scots. Even the cynical capitalism that motivated the railway building celebrated in *The Iron Horse* is disguised in historical romance.

To Ford, history is society at work; in retrospect, and with the inconsistencies ironed out, he presents it as an example of the logical order to which we should aspire in our own lives. He chooses for his settings periods when the merits of the social system—emotional security, a collective strength, the virtue of living by basic moral values—are most notably on show; wars, and especially their conclusion in defeat or Pyrrhic victory; a time when minor parts of society—the Seventh Cavalry, the Irish, the sharecroppers of Kansas, a lost patrol in the Mesopotamian desert, even individuals like Mary Queen of Scots—are cut off and must fend for themselves, sustained only by beliefs the system has inculcated. Even under the most intolerable pressure, the structure stands, and is reinforced by adversity. Mary's cry to Elizabeth "Still, still I win," Ma Joad's "We're the people who live; ain't nothing gonna stop us," Ford's use of the triumphal "Battle Hymn of the Republic" over the most massive scenes of military defeat show that something essential in the spirit of social man can never be destroyed, if only he will believe, affirm, keep faith.

THE FORD HERO

Characters in Ford's films work under a strong disadvantage; deprived of individuality in favour of embodying the virtues of a society, they are types rather than people, and as they cannot alter without casting doubt on the virtues they represent, their personalities remain frozen in time. There is a tendency for characters to slip in and out of the story rather than hold the centre of the stage throughout, and most stories derive their drama from bringing together two existing opposites rather than showing an individual changing under stress. The problem is exacerbated by Ford's habit of casting a person in similar roles in a number of his films, a method that, while exploiting the accumulated audience response to a familiar face, also narrows the range of interpretation available to an actor. The bluff honesty of Ward Bond, Hank Worden's Shakespearean idiocy, the courteous chivalry of Harry Carey swing on close acquaintance perilously close to *cliché*, without, nonetheless, ever slipping over. That they do not is a tribute to Ford's genius in the manipulation of his self-limited materials, and to his obvious love of the types that leads us to respond with affection rather than irritation to Victor McLaglen's eternal Irish bruiser or Jack Pennick's ubiquitous barman, labourer or man in the ranks.

Given these restrictions, the role of hero in a Ford film is strewn with difficulties. He must embody the virtues of his society and yet be remote enough from it to register as an individual; must be, as well, a hero while suggesting that society neither respects nor admires people who are not content to live by its rules but must lead, defy, dominate. Although Ford needs such men to provide the focuses of his more ambitious statements, he implies that the greatest heroes are those who do not realise their importance but, like Marty Maher, the West Point functionary of *The Long Grey Line,* and Samuel Mudd, *The Prisoner of Shark Island,* influence others by a life of good example or selfless fortitude in the face of injustice.

Left : "Weakness and Vulnerability"—
John Wayne in SHE WORE A YELLOW RIBBON

Below : Henry Fonda stands with "clear-eyed directness" at the back of the crowd in THE GRAPES OF WRATH

Acknowledging the contradictions of his approach, Ford makes most of his heroes outsiders, chronic wanderers who accept the necessity of serving society, admire its virtues, secretly wish to be part of it but are driven by personal motives to reject its security. Occasionally a Ford film shows a man settling down, but more often the last shot is of him marching, riding or walking on, accepting with resignation his burden as scapegoat and saviour. Society needs its heroes, but when the danger is past they must be ejected lest they endanger the smooth working of the social machine. These transitional figures accept the stigma of all heroes since the beginning of society, and their characters often have mythical or Biblical overtones. Expiators of society's guilt or solvers of its problems, they are also prophets and guides, mystical forerunners of mankind's next development. Most often, they are neither pious nor strong, but mere men doing what they must in response to drives that eclipse their feelings. Ethan Edwards in *The Searchers* and Tom Joad in *The Grapes of Wrath* are their most memorable incarnations, but few Ford films lack such characters. The men played by John Wayne are especially close to Ford's ideal of self-sacrifice; the last bandit in *Three Godfathers* tormented by visions, staggering blindly out of the desert with the baby, Nathan Brittles in *She Wore a Yellow Ribbon* ignoring his retirement to return and fulfil a promise as Ringo in *Stagecoach* achieves the vow to kill his brother's murderers. Ford sensed in Wayne's persona the core of weakness, of vulnerability that has led to him being cast often in roles involving his defeat or death. (The present eminence of "Big John" disguises the fact that in his early career he was a stock "other man" who got killed in the last reel, leaving the heroine to his buddy; cf. *The Fighting Seebees*, *The Sands of Iwo Jima*, *Reap the Wild Wind*). One finds this mood of helpless subjection to inner needs even in small Ford roles like the pathetic child rapist Sayer (Laurence Naismith) in *Gideon of Scotland Yard*, left alone in the house with a little girl and agonisingly unable to resist the urge that sends him slowly upstairs to her room, or, more ambitiously the doctor (William Holden) of *The Horse*

Soldiers who, despite the risk of imprisonment and death, remains in enemy territory to treat the wounded.

Henry Fonda, not so vulnerable as Wayne, more independent and with a studied insolence that Wayne also lacks, has been less often in Ford's favour, and not at all since the production of *Mr. Roberts* in 1955, when director and star had a violent disagreement over interpretation that ended their partnership. With Fonda, Ford preferred to concentrate on the mystical aspect of the hero, and to cast him in roles implying a dedication to higher ideals rather than the innate restlessness that drives his other wanderers. Tom Joad leaves his family to spread the gospel of social reform, the priest in *The Fugitive*, a thinly-disguised Christ figure, suffers and dies for the church, Abe Lincoln in *Young Mr. Lincoln* discards his law practice to change the structure of American history, Colonel Thursday in *Fort Apache* sacrifices himself in an affirmation of the military tradition by which he has always lived. Fonda's clear-eyed directness is in sharp contrast to Wayne's expression of wounded pride and the frowning likability of Ward Bond, but all are related in their rejection of conventional social roles, their subjection to rigid personal codes of conduct, their restless search for the perfect life that will never eventuate, since the instant it is offered they turn away.

FORD AND STYLE

Any discussion of the Ford style is in danger of falling into the same trap as analysis of his films, since his regular use of certain situations and pictorial effects can obscure the varying emotional and dramatic importance these have from film to film. Some of these are familiar enough to be trademarks; the taste for slanting morning or afternoon light, for arches and doors in shooting which the screen's centre is illuminated and the outer areas dark, the use of filters to accentuate clouds, and a detached camera style of which the exterior mid-shot with the camera pointing slightly downwards is the most important component. But mere accumulation of themes gives little insight into Ford's films, since an image that in one production may

The slanting morning light of TOBACCO ROAD

be a symbol of immense weight can become in another nothing more than a detail, just as a dance in *Fort Apache* conveys an entirely different meaning to one in *My Darling Clementine*. The "door" set-up that opens and closes *The Searchers* is, for that film, a powerful symbolic motif referred to often as the film goes on, always to comment on the central conflict of family versus the wandering hero, whereas in *The Fugitive*, where an early shot shows the priest moving through a shadowy arch to approach his old village, it is a mere

gesture, considerably less important than Ford's manipulation of Catholic images and of shadows. Even identical scenes and lines of dialogue can have widely contrasting effects in different films. When Ford repeats in *Two Rode Together* the scene from *My Darling Clementine* where Wyatt Earp orders out of town a gambler who arrives on the stage, allowing him only the courtesy of a meal and a wash, the gestures, despite similarities that extend even to the same foot-on-post pose, are total opposites in effect, as different as the men who make them. An exchange that for Earp was an exercise in his newly-won authority is for Guthrie McCabe a mere autocratic twitch, deprived of meaning since it lacks the preceding proof of moral worth Earp offered in his subjugation of the drunken Indian who was terrorising the town.

Nor can a simple thematic approach to Ford's imagery handle the apparent contradictions of *The Informer* and *The Fugitive*, both of which replace the flat, detached camerawork of later films with looming low-angle close-ups and an almost Expressionist use of artificial lighting, concentrate on interiors to the total exclusion of landscape and rely heavily on formal symbology. So aggressive is the style of these films that only a similarity in attitude and morality appears to link them to the bulk of Ford's work, but such an assumption misunderstands the essential spirit of Ford's Westerns. The visual style of *The Informer* is not qualitatively different to *She Wore a Yellow Ribbon*, since in both cases Ford chooses his location for its theatrical value more than for historical appropriateness, and relates every aspect of the landscape to some moral concept or conflict; as in *The Informer* the dark streets and fog of Dublin reflect Gypo's state of mind, so the mesas of Monument Valley are intimately involved with the issues of his cavalry films. Ford's style is essentially a theatrical one. Among his films, his personal favourites

Opposite : three of Ford's notable shots. Top left : Henry Fonda in MY DARLING CLEMENTINE. Top right : Pedro Armendariz in THREE GODFATHERS. Bottom : The deputy in TWO RODE TOGETHER

have always been the most artificial in style— *Young Mr. Lincoln, The Sun Shines Bright*, most recently *The Fugitive*—suggesting that extravagant pictorialism can be connoted with deep intellectual and emotional involvement on Ford's part. He claims he never saw *My Darling Clementine* and of *They Were Expendable* remarked (astonishingly) "I just can't believe that picture's any good"; such statements can only be accepted if one sees Ford as essentially an intellectual moralist who regards as his best work that in which the point is expressed with greatest force and dramatic value. His quieter films, of which *My Darling Clementine* and *They Were Expendable* are typical, suggest a more personal and unbuttoned Ford, from which he prefers, for the record, to be disassociated.

The essence of Ford's style lies in an extremely specific and symbolic manipulation of gestures, visual situations and landscape, and his personal signature is in his rearrangement of these in relation to his characters to create meaningful contrasts between them. As long as his collaborators respect these finely judged contrasts, he seems content to allow cameramen and writers a remarkable degree of licence. As a result, few directors have suffered so painfully at the hands of studio technical departments, which regularly mutilate his films by adding extra footage or inappropriate music. (It is worth remembering, however, that Ford's memory of such situations is open to doubt. He recalls inserted close-ups in *The Iron Horse* where none appear, exaggerates the details of a chase where he was forced to be his own stunt man in *North of Hudson Bay* and is excessively critical of Max Steiner's subtle score for *The Searchers* while accepting with equanimity Richard Hageman's universally deplored music for *The Fugitive*.) "Get a good cameraman," he advised young directors. "He knows more about a camera than you'll ever know," and elsewhere, "I never had an argument with a photographer." Such remarks are typical of Ford's attitude to his collaborators. As long as they accept his requirements as to certain specific effects, he is content to let them go their own way. The "Ford camera style" of his Monument Valley films is as much Winton Hoch as Ford, while the signature of Joe August and Gregg Toland is equally strong on the films they shot for him. It is futile to look for the Ford style in a unique way of moving the camera, or of editing, since the real consistency is in the thread of character and the pattern of visual language, both of which he respects utterly, and follows with total disregard for visual consistency. Throughout Ford's films open exteriors alternate with artificial interiors, genuine darkness with obvious day-for-night shooting without thought for the jarring effect on the viewer, but studio shooting is less often an example of false economy than an effort by Ford to gain a specific effect of lighting, the disconcerting disappearance of a character dictated by the necessity to continue the development of an idea, a lapse of dialogue indicating not a lack of invention but a decision to employ his highly developed sense of significant gesture and his poetic view of landscape to say things that words cannot convey.

The importance Ford assigns to this precise balance of effects is dramatised nowhere more effectively than in *The Searchers*, in a sequence where the search party prepares to creep into the Indian camp at night to rescue the hostages. Ford shoots the scene from the top of a Monument Valley cliff, showing the Indian camp in the valley below, its fires winking, and outlining the figure of Martin Pawley on the cliff edge as he crawls down and into the village on a scouting mission. Of the many ways to organise such a sequence, Ford's was surely the most complex. The footage was shot as "day for night," ie. exposed by sunlight but with filters over the lens to simulate darkness. To suggest the camp-fires, which would not have been visible through filters, Ford used mirrors whose light was flashed up to the hill by dozens of extras in the camp. Alternation of angles must have made the shot both difficult and dangerous, since the cliff on which it is set is steep. A sequence that the average director would have done painlessly in a few hours occupied Ford, one estimates, about two days, and involved some highly complex second-unit direction and camera-work, an effort justified by the precise effects he gained of Martin silhouetted against the night sky, of the Indian village cradled in the valley, intimately related to its landscape, of the inter-relation of night and the danger of the enterprise.

FORD AND WRITERS

Although it appears contradictory that Ford, who achieves his effects by careful use of action and gesture, should have relied on scenarists, learned much from them and developed an imagery almost totally literary in its basis, such relationships are common in arts that relate to the cinema and Ford's kind of film. The great church painters of the early Renaissance, men who, like Ford, needed to combine a moral lesson with attractive popular art, had philosophers and theologians provide for their works detailed "plots" that dictated the precise placement of the various figures, their clothing and expressions. Composers of opera, a form which much of the American cinema closely resembles, take their text from librettists who, though often without great literary ability, have a special talent for dialogue that blends with and enhances the music, adding to it an additional dramatic power. (Whitman was devoted to Italian opera, and acknowledged its influence on his work.) To accept that Ford depends on his scenarists is not to deprecate his talent but rather to understand that the greatest non-verbal artists often need the sounding board of a verbal dimension in order to focus their statement.

Ford chose, trained, influenced and relied upon his best writers; two of them, Frank Nugent and Dudley Nichols, between them receive credits on twenty-four of his features, while Nunnally Johnson, Frank Wead, James Kevin McGuinness and Lamar Trotti are represented on three or four films each. These men, all of whom had an instinctive understanding of Ford's style, and particularly Nichols, who played an important part in forming it, provided Ford with a depth to his work that eluded him in the silent period, a heightened sense of drama that for the first time allowed him to give

simple incidents the same emotional significance as character confrontations, and to capture in dialogue the vitality previously
confined to scenes of action. Nichols was an especially valuable find,
an ex-newsman and playwright whom Ford discovered for the
submarine drama *Men without Women* in 1930. "From then on,"
Ford said, "we worked together as much as possible, and I worked
very closely with him. He had never written a script before, but he
was very good, and he had the same idea I had about paucity of
dialogue." In the light of this statement, the *Sequence* dismissal of
Nichols is manifestly unjustified, though consistent with its critical
stand on Ford. The most notable fault in its attitude to the Nichols/
Ford collaboration is summed up in a passage where Lindsay
Anderson isolates those aspects of *The Fugitive* he regards as
unsatisfactory and, *ipso facto*, imposed by Nichols; the faults—"a
sentimental simplification of issues and characters, a highly self-
conscious striving for significance, and a fundamental unreality"—
are precisely the features that, stripped of pejorative adjectives,
emerge as Ford's greatest virtues. Leaving aside critical objections
to the statement, is it likely that as individual an artist as Ford would
have endured for fourteen films a collaborator who imposed on his
work characteristics that marred its value and blunted its point? To
assume so is once again to sell Ford, as man and artist, substantially
short.

Ford's continuing debt to Nichols is dramatised by his later use of
many details developed in his association with the writer. The gesture
of the police chief in *The Informer* in pushing Gypo's reward towards
him with a pencil, an action Nichols acknowledged as his invention
and a visual symbol of contempt, recurs in *Fort Apache* (Frank
Nugent) where Thursday picks up an Indian head-dress with his
pencil, and in *How Green Was My Valley* (Philip Dunne) in which
the teacher indicates his distaste for Huw by pushing off the boy's
cap with a cane. Despite different writers, Ford has retained both
the gesture and, more important, the specific dramatic meaning
Nichols assigned to it.

Nichols's few published statements about screenwriting show a scenarist in the self-conscious tradition of Hollywood in the Thirties, drawn equally to the fashionable dramatic conventions of Broadway and the universality of the popular cinema. One senses that he regarded Hollywood films as second-rate theatre, but was prepared to work hard at injecting into them the basic theatrical values as a means of improving their flaccid intellectual tone. He saw the screenwriter as an independent creative artist collaborating with the director rather than serving him, and his job as providing a formal pattern for the director's visual and dramatic efforts. Much of his work he clearly felt to be over the heads of the audience, making its point almost subliminally. Speaking of *The Informer,* he proudly revealed the symbolism of the poster, the blind man and the fog, details instantly understood by Ford and employed with varying degrees of dramatic weight. Ford humoured his collaborator, incorporating even his most extreme flights of fancy, providing they did not intrude on his meaning, and was eventually influenced by Nichols's method. Clearly Nichols did not truly understand his relationship to Ford, but this does not diminish its importance.

With Nichols's help, Ford brought his work indoors. The uneven adventure stories of the silent period were replaced by a new kind of drama in which Ford combined action with ideas in a totally new way. His Thirties films are not merely expansions of his silent productions but works in a new and more sophisticated filmic language, admitting the assistance of talented collaborators and dealing with issues that could not have been tackled with his direct but simple silent style. Nichols, recognising that Ford told his stories not in terms of character development but rather by bringing characters of opposite values into conflict, and noting that the director shared his dislike for the brisk dialogue style fashionable at the time, conceived sequences and whole films in terms of significant mood, gestures and individual actions, a system Ford instantly adopted. His taste ran instinctively to symbolic imagery, a reflection of his Catholic background, and he was familiar with a visual language in which

Henry Fonda, John Ford and Cathy Downs on the set of
MY DARLING CLEMENTINE

virtues and attitudes were embodied in actions and even objects; wrath shown by a storm, peace in a tranquil sea, holiness symbolised by a visible aura, innocence by the attitude of prayer, virtue by the modestly draped and bowed head of the madonna. As he explored and developed his skill during the Thirties, he found ways to extend this arbitrary and essentially literary symbology into every part of his work. From a mere background to his stories, the visible world developed into a reflection of the drama's moral issues, with land-scape chosen and manipulated to provide a commentary on his theme, natural events like storms related, as in *The Hurricane*, to a specific application of divine wrath, or, as in *Mary of Scotland*, to disordered mental processes. By continued precise application, purely decorative effects accumulated a symbolic meaning; the human shadow and silhouette to convey death or the threat of it, rivers to represent peace, dust dissolution. Although the sources of these symbols are demonstrably Catholic and literary, Ford's application of them as part of a consistent visual style became the cornerstone of his claim to be considered as a genius of the cinema.

FORD AND CATHOLICISM

Ford's adherence to the Roman Catholic religion in which he was educated is so pronounced in all aspects of his films that one is surprised it is so little commented on, though the reason is obviously connected with the assumption that a director of Ford's presumed devotion to American principles should, if he professed any religion at all, follow some flinty New England Fundamentalism. Fordian Catholicism is regarded as social rather than spiritual, his nod towards the infinite or a minor detail used to add colour to Irish comedies and, as such, rather less important a factor than the use of the Irish Jig. In fact the Catholic religion is pivotal to Ford's work, eclipsing even his devotion to military life, which in his films is tinged with religious observance. Many of his war-time casualties are martyrs who die for a cause beyond military victory, while incidents like the habit of officers at funerals addressing the Almighty as "Sir" and adopting military terminology for their remarks over the dead, as well as the conclusion of *What Price Glory?* where Ford makes the explicit comparison of the profession of arms and a rigorous religion, show how even the strongest forces in his character are subsidiary to direct and emotional moral convictions.

On all levels of Ford's work, Catholic dogma, philosophy and imagery play an important role. At the most basic, religious morality affects his choice of plots; speaking of sexual subjects, he remarked "they would be against my nature, my religion and my natural inclinations." A powerful religious conscience is apparent in his selection of the moral lessons for which his films are always vehicles.

All of these reflect Catholic thinking. He supports the concept of a "just war" in favour of the American liberal view best synopsised as "War is hell, but . . .," assigns to large social groups a collective piety, implies in all deaths the existence of an afterlife, accentuated by his habit of bringing back the dead, either in concluding flashbacks, or by implication in the form of portraits, themselves imitative of religious images; the quasi-devotional offering of flowers before portraits of women is common in his films, yet another aspect of his veneration of the Virgin Mary. His films abound in such acts of religious ritual, reflecting or relating to those of the Catholic church; the Bible as a focus for family discipline is given due weight, attributions of divine guidance or intervention are frequent, many of his older characters have religious or quasi-religious standing—bishops, priests, "elders." Beyond this, his imagery, as later chapters indicate, is overtly Catholic in its source, drawing on the familiar visual language of religious art, but adding to it his own unique pictorial metaphors. This language, with which this book mainly deals, is the basis of Ford's work, and an understanding of it central to an awareness of his genius.

*   *   *

Should Ford be examined in this way? Or does textual criticism merely confuse our response to the most obvious component of his films, their superb value as entertainment? The best argument in favour of this approach is a consistency between the language of Ford's films and his own values, expressed and implied; such a consistency cannot be doubted.* Ford's resistance to the label of a serious film-maker has counted most against a true evaluation of his work in modern critical terms. The extreme artistic statements of a Welles, a Bergman or a von Sternberg encourage a reaction on the part of critics, and in the conflict a balance is established. But Ford, wary of exposing his views or the underlying message of his work, appears to make no statements, either in person or on film, presenting

* This book is not a study of Ford's entire work but an examination of Ford's filmic language and its use in some of his more important films.

C

himself as a simple entertainer concerned only to do his humble best. Confused, we retreat into reverence or disinterest. If Ford had Visconti's idiosyncratic choice of subjects or expressed himself as forcibly as does Godard, we could accept him as the superior director he undoubtedly is, but his reticence leaves us guessing. One wants to respect his artistic privacy, and would do so in the case of a lesser talent. But is "He Made Westerns" sufficient an epitaph for one of the greatest artists the cinema has produced?

John Ford visiting Howard Hawks and Michele Carey on location for EL DORADO

2. Some Silents: Cameo Kirby, North of Hudson Bay, Three Bad Men

Unlike his sound career, which is relatively consistent in artistic and commercial success, Ford's film-making during the middle and late Twenties shows three logical stages. After his apprenticeship with his brother Francis as assistant director, actor and stunt-man, he graduated to directing two-reel Westerns for Universal, many starring Harry Carey, and although he alternated shorter films with some five-reelers, including *Straight Shooting* (1917), his first feature, there was little qualitative difference among the films he directed up until the early Twenties, while the few examples one has been able to view of his work in this period suggest that, although Ford was already exhibiting his mastery of outdoor action and natural locations, it was a skill he shared with many other directors of the time. The Mustang two-reelers of William Wyler in particular show a taste for atmospheric outdoor shooting and camera movement that equals Ford's.

In 1920 Ford directed *Hitchin' Posts*, a five-reel Civil War melodrama with Frank Mayo as a southern aristocrat turned professional riverboat card-sharp. Three years later, by this time having moved to Fox where facilities and budgets were more generous, Ford re-made the story as *Cameo Kirby*, his first film as "John" rather than "Jack" Ford, and one showing a Ford quite different from that of the Universal days. His eight features for Fox prior to *The Iron Horse* (1924) are the second important phase of his career, but the shortage of available prints and the poor quality of many that do survive makes it difficult to analyse the nature of Ford's development. His style and approach changed considerably in the graduation from simple two-reelers. A new photographic richness was apparent, stemming from his partnership with the brilliant cinematographer George Schneiderman, who was to shoot most of Ford's Fox films, and with whom Ford was to establish a *rapport* similar to that achieved with Joseph August in his early sound films, with Gregg Toland on his more serious dramas and with Winton Hoch on the outdoor romances of the Fifties. With this richness came a stiffness and theatricality of style, but as well a growing emphasis on actions as a guide to personality. More and more frequently his films became subtle examinations of character rather than pure adventure stories, and an interest in significant gestures, both physical and moral, increasingly characterised Ford's work.

Cameo Kirby (1923) shows how completely Ford's films had matured since his days with Carey, and how strongly that change tended towards formality and the development of an emotionally charged directorial language. John Gilbert plays John "Cameo" Kirby, a Southern gentleman driven by his involvement in an accidental killing to become a professional gambler on the Mississippi river-boats. Having fallen in love with Adele Randall (Gertrude Olmstead), the daughter of Colonel Randall (William Lawrence), owner of a large plantation, he eases himself into a poker game between Randall and the crooked Colonel Moreau (Alan Hale) in order to win back the plantation out of which Moreau has cheated the Colonel. However, just as Kirby is knocking on his door to return the deed to his land, Randall shoots himself, leaving a letter naming Kirby as the cause of his downfall. Kirby is pondering this on deck a few minutes later when Moreau tries to shoot him. Wounded, he falls overboard, is rescued by a friend, regains his health, tracks down Moreau, kills him in a gun duel and, after misunderstandings brought on by the efforts of Moreau's confederates to discredit him, is united with Adele.

For all its incidental beauty and relevance to Ford's later work, at least in theme, *Cameo Kirby* is far from a total success, although the opening scenes on the Mississippi with a beautifully photographed river-boat race almost identical with that in *Steamboat Round the*

John Gilbert and Gertrude Olmstead in a scene from
CAMEO KIRBY

Bend (1935)—the later film even uses some of the same footage—show Ford's theatrical mastery of outdoor locations and his affection for the vanished elegance of the old South. Negro slaves strum banjos under the trees as the boats come by; Adele Randall and her friend Ann (Jean Arthur) hurry in crinolines through a wood to see the end of the race; Kirby and Adele meet by the well amid cooing doves, her first glimpse of him as a quivering reflection in the water, a Byronic figure swathed in a cape with the cameos that give him his nickname glowing at neck and wrists. The film's vision of the South suggests a period fantasy rather than the sun-baked lassitude of Mark Twain's river-boat world, while its brief depiction of New Orleans in a flashback where Kirby describes the killing that made him a fugitive is as unreal as the London of *The Long Voyage Home*; a cobbled tropical port with sailors dancing a bizarre hornpipe and bars inhabited by knife-wielding bandits in eye-patches and earrings. Few critics who measure Ford's films by the epic standards of *The Searchers* and *The Grapes of Wrath* would find much common ground with this formalised and highly artificial romance, but in attitude and acting style some similarities to Ford's later work are apparent.

Still not the master he was later to become of dialogue and its enlivening by careful pacing, Ford reduces the last half of the film to a tedious set of interior conversations that could have been directed by anybody. The camera remains rigidly fixed except for some tracking shots in the early scenes of pursuit, Ford choosing to dwell on formalised photographic images to capitalise on the romance of his characters. But in using gestures suggestive of his characters' personalities, Ford already shows his ability. Gilbert was carefully schooled to make every movement relate to his role of the wandering aristocrat, doomed never to find his peace; the cavalier way he handles money, tossing down a bag of gold as Ethan Edwards does in *The Searchers* decades later, and his casual use of his silver-topped cane, rapping preemptorily on doors or sliding it under his arm in a gesture that telegraphs instantly his breeding, could not be bettered as indices to character. His duel with Moreau in a wind-swept grove is perfectly directed, the wind giving to the otherwise undramatic background a heightened reality and a sense that the elements are reflecting the emotions of those who fight. The slanting light used for almost all his exteriors and the effect of sunlight on dust when Ford shoots along an avenue of trees down which riders gallop to arrest Kirby are attractive visual effects, although in general the landscape is not capitalised upon.

There is an equal degree of contrivance in the film that followed *Cameo Kirby*, *North of Hudson Bay* (1923), but this is less of a success. Starring Tom Mix as a rancher who visits northern Canada to look for his miner brother, only to find him murdered by claim-jumpers and himself almost their victim, it was shot at Yosemite, mostly in dead of winter, with patently unreal glass-shots supplying the towering mountains of the Yukon. Mix, popular at the time as "The Well-Dressed Cowboy," makes a believable job of Michael Dane, the young midwest rancher who obviously occupies a lesser place in his old mother's heart than his more adventurous brother Peter (Eugene Pallette), but who nevertheless obeys her request to find her boy. His early scenes in the ranch house, comforting his aged, Ma Joad-like mother, convey through Ford's subtle use of gesture and movement a remarkable sense of Michael's inferior position and the eminence of the unseen brother, as well as the motivation that drives him to travel thousands of miles in search of him. As lost and as subject to the call of duty as any of Ford's more important heroes in later films, Michael Dane gains from Mix's playing a charming vulnerability, especially evident in the steamer sequence where, penned up in one bare, white-walled cabin with an old Indian woman, two nuns, a mocking Mountie and Estelle MacDonald (Kathleen Key), he tries, with great difficulty, to make himself agreeable to the girl. It is typical of Ford that Michael should do this by trading in sign language with the old Indian for her fur beret in order to give it to Estelle, and that the deal should be consummated when he offers the former his shaving set as a trade;

the reliance on gesture, the concept of trade as a basic vehicle for understanding, the characterisation of Indians as amiable simpletons with little personality of their own, even courtship by ritual gift (the theme of *The Quiet Man*) all recur frequently in Ford's later films.

Like *Cameo Kirby* and many other Ford silents before the epic period of *The Iron Horse* and *Three Bad Men,* the action highlights of *North of Hudson Bay* suffer by comparison with the stiffness of the plotted sequences, in the case of this film a tedious piece of mechanical story-telling that involves Estelle's evil trader uncle (Frank Campeau) rigging a rifle in his office to go off when a concentrated beam of sunlight ignites the powder in the breach, a device that kills Michael's brother and later the trader himself. In each case the suspect, first Peter's partner Angus (Will Walling) and then Michael, is sentenced to the unlikely justice of being hounded from settlement to settlement, deprived of food and shelter until he dies. Both are saved when, after a hand-to-hand fight with a wolf pack and a perilous canoe chase down a half-frozen stream, Estelle reveals her uncle's plot, but the whole idea is so preposterous that one never takes it seriously. One remembers moments of immense visual clarity, gestures that sum up in instant visual short-hand a complex situation, and although *North of Hudson Bay* is relatively barren of these, the shot where, as Michael and Angus carefully coax a fire from their last match, the foot of an Indian pursuer appears instantly to crush it out in the snow, makes acceptable for one moment the total implausibility of the elaborate plot.

After a further programme melodrama, *Hoodman Blind* (1924), Ford made a film that was to change his career and concentrate those aspects of his until—then disorganised style later to become typical of him. *The Iron Horse* (1924), powerful, direct, integrating history with human activity, creating in the character of Davy Brandon (George O'Brien) a perfect symbol of the American capitalist fervour and expansionist energy that built the huge railroads of the 1860s, was the first of Ford's films to draw attention to him as a stylist, though his obvious affection for the epic subject, his skilful use of weather and landscape and the dramatic effectiveness of natural disasters like the buffalo stampede that nearly overwhelms the builders contributed to the categorisation that haunted Ford for the next forty years. While it's idle to deny that Ford is a great outdoor director and *The Iron Horse* one of his masterpieces, it is equally wrong to suggest that all his exterior films show the same flourish and epic scope as this early success, whose subject and underlying significance clearly moved Ford deeply.

The epic, like the comedy, can be romantic or socially conscious, rely on character or action, dialogue or mime. Nothing dramatises this more effectively than Ford's *Three Bad Men* (1926), one of his

John Ford (at right) in position to film the buffalo stampede for THE IRON HORSE. Cameramen—George Schneiderman and Burnett Guffey

most important yet largely unknown dramas of the silent period. Again starring George O'Brien, this time playing Dan O'Malley, a young cowpoke and relatively minor character, *Three Bad Men* has a charm, visual precision, even an intimacy that many of Ford's more ambitious outdoor films lack. A series of related incidents set around the Dakota land rush of the 1880s and the boom town of Custer, it is less an integrated story than a tapestry of action through which weave the connecting threads of an attempt by the evil sheriff of Custer, Layne Hunter, (Lou Tellegen) to capitalise on the land rush, the love affair between Dan O'Malley and Lee Carlton (Olive Borden) and the intervention of three sentimental bandits, Mike Costigan (J. Farrell McDonald), Bull Stanley (Tom Santschi) and Spade Allen (Frank Campeau) in both situations, first to thwart Hunter, then to bring together the lovers. Motivation for their acts is provided by Hunter's corrupt administration of the town; he protects the gangsters who kill Lee Carlton's father, condones the burning down of the church set up by an itinerant minister (Alec B. Francis) and finally murders Bull Stanley's sister, a "fallen woman" and one of Hunter's string of dancing girls. When the land rush begins, the bad men sacrifice themselves one by one to delay Hunter's gang, until Davy shoots the sheriff in a final gun-battle. Although the land rush sequence is not really the point of the film, occupying only one reel, its visual bravura remains impressive despite later attempts to equal its scope with films like *Cimarron*; the crescent of wagons drawn up on the salt flat, around which Ford pans proudly at one point to prove there is no fakery, the intricate cutting from soldiers holding back the group to the gun crew staring at their watches, the quiver of excitement that runs through the settlers, the children, even their animals—then the eruption of action that sweeps across the dusty plain, wagons overturned and splintering, a penny-farthing bicycle towed behind a horse, a couple unwittingly leaving their baby behind as they stop to replace a wheel, and the child whipped out of harm's way by a suddenly appearing hand, the travelling newspaperman printing his broadsheets as his wagon thunders across the plain; this complex alternation of graphic individual scenes gives a more powerful if disorganised impression of the event than later CinemaScope recreations of it.

A conventional thematic analysis of *Three Bad Men* would place it, with *The Iron Horse* and *Stagecoach*, as one of Ford's American-style adventure stories, incorporating as it does the familiar elements of the wagon train, the cavalry, the conflict between farmer and fighter. It is even accessible, like many Westerns by Anthony Mann and William Wellman, in terms of landscape contrasts; the plain belongs to peace and security, the mountains that loom in the background, setting for the final gunfights, to strife and sudden death. Yet to concentrate on any of these factors is to ignore much that gives the film its richness, especially the religious imagery that dominates many important sequences. Ford returns to the trinity motif central to the *Three Godfathers* story, which he made twice (*Marked Men,* 1919, *Three Godfathers,* 1948) and referred to often in other films, and *Three Bad Men,* like all these, has powerful echoes of Catholic doctrine. As in *Three Godfathers,* the three heroes sacrifice themselves to protect the innocent, in their case an orphaned baby, and, in defying the guilty, affirm the final triumph of good. Supporting this theme with some concise visual clues, Ford tells the story as a series of ritual acts, many dominated by religious images; the old minister, shot down before his church, dies with the burning cross behind him; carrying his dead sister, Millie, Bull pauses on the stairs in an expressive pose of holy wrath and sorrow reminiscent of the traditional *pietà.* The arrival of the priest, alighting wearily from the coach and then washing himself in a ritual lustration, the immediate announcement by Millie Stanley to Layne Hunter that they can now get married, even Hunter's rejection of this request by sliding closed a panel identical with that of a confessional are gestures that convey a sense of allegorical conflict conceived in terms of Christian elements, to which the Lucifer combination of pure white clothing and physical beauty in Hunter, and the Father, Son and Holy Ghost trinity of the bad men point constantly. The issue is

summed up with extraordinary power in the film's final shot, where, as the ghosts of the three are seen riding off into the sunset, all hold out their arms in a stylised representation of the crucifixion. Here the familiar Ford connotation of the skyline shot with death, already used in *Three Bad Men* when, on the trio's first appearance, he dissolves from a "Wanted" poster to their sinister silhouettes coming out of the sun, is brilliantly traded upon as Ford adopts familiar imagery from religious art to suggest both death and resurrection.

The importance of shadow imagery to Ford's work is worth pursuing beyond the limited space allowed in this book. In a linkage that is typical of his work, Ford connotes a human shadow or silhouette with death; they are literally "shades" from the other world. This is evident not only in his choice of skyline shots to foreshadow death, but in his precise use of half-shadow to refer to the great dead, especially Lincoln, who is seen slumped beyond a curtain in *The Prisoner of Shark Island* and outlined on a hilltop in *Young Mr. Lincoln*. Dedicating *Three Godfathers* to Harry Carey, "bright star of the early western sky," who died during the film's production, he showed a horseman outlined on a desert hill against the evening sun. Dying Doc Holliday in *My Darling Clementine* silhouetted against a starry sky or glowing window; Peabody in *The Man Who Shot Liberty Valance* whose shadow on the wall presages his savage beating by the men who wait in the dark; Tom and Casey in *The Grapes of Wrath* pursuing a dying community across the twilit rim of the world; mourners gathered at the pit-head in *How Green Was My Valley* as the dead are brought up; sailors on the "Glencairn" silent at the rail as Yank is buried at sea in *The Long Voyage Home*; although setting and characters change, the symbol and its power do not.

The flexibility with which Ford can play on this device is shown in contrasting scenes from *The Searchers* and *She Wore a Yellow Ribbon*; in *The Searchers*, a child, hiding in the family graveyard,

Three of Ford's silhouette shots. Top left : THE GRAPES OF WRATH. Top right : THE LONG VOYAGE HOME. Bottom : THREE GODFATHERS

looks up in terror as the shadow of an Indian falls across her, a purely dramatic gesture that rhymes with the graveyard setting to suggest the horror of the child's situation and her imminent death, at least in the sense of her relationship with the community. (Her uncle Ethan later dismisses her after adoption of Indian ways as "dead" and attempts twice to kill her.) Yet in Nathan Brittles's quiet soliloquy to his wife on her grave in *She Wore a Yellow Ribbon*, the sudden appearance of Olivia Pennell's shadow, rising up the stone like a reincarnation of the dead woman, conveys with an almost identical visual device a remarkable sense of continuity with the past ("She's a lot like you," Brittles has already mused to the ghost of his wife), suggesting that, despite death, the community will survive in its young people, a strong theme in this beautiful film.

A familiarity with Ford's regular and consistent use of this device gives added depth to *Three Bad Men*, and we can see more clearly the essential drama of shots as that at the beginning of *The Fugitive*, where the priest enters his old church and his shadow on the floor forms the cross of the crucifixion. It is not a Gothic or Expressionist use of shadows to add "atmosphere" but a literal (and literary) connotation of the human shadow with death and the after-life similar to Ford's use of the storm as a symbol of mental turmoil in *Young Mr. Lincoln* and *She Wore a Yellow Ribbon*, and wind as a metaphor of sexual passion in *The Quiet Man* and *The Long Voyage Home*. For the same reason, Ford's comparison of fog and Gypo's mental state in *The Informer* is less an imposition of extraneous symbolic detail by Dudley Nichols than a consistent exploration by both he and Ford of the specific literary imagery used in other films. Lindsay Anderson's stress on the universal appeal of Ford's work is justifiable in this respect, that the basis of his imagery is so rooted in the common experience and broadly agreed symbology of art and literature that its appeal to us is on the instinctive and emotional level, not the intellectual. For this reason it cannot be enjoyed half-heartedly or with a sense of patronage; it is too honest and unguarded for that, and so must we be if we hope to derive from Ford's films the devout and affectionate feeling for God and man with which he fills them.

*　　*　　*

The confidence of Ford's visual style and the skill with which it was used often sagged in his silent work, though its peaks in films like *Three Bad Men,* where the adventure is stiffened with moral purpose, sometimes disguised this. In discussing his silent films, one must frequently single out individual action sequences—the duel in *Cameo Kirby,* the buffalo stampede in *The Iron Horse*—and pass over the dull dialogue scenes of the first and the waxworks stiffness of the political tableaux that preface the railroad building in the other. A further, related fault was his tendency within action sequences to rely on an artificial method of construction and editing more descriptive than evocative. In the land rush of *Three Bad Men,* the flicking camera, darting from details of a boy and his dog to the humorous incidents of the race and back to a panoramic view often neutralised the sweep of the incident which a moving camera and a more generalised view might have retained. There is, in fact, too much story in this sequence, and not enough in the more appropriate dialogue scenes, where it really belongs. This lack of balance, combined with Ford's disinterest in character development (as opposed to conflict) and the resulting arbitrary disappearance of individuals from the story for long periods, marred some of his later silents, and it was not until the sound era and his collaboration with a number of talented screenwriters that Ford found the ideal method of blending his *penchant* for character analysis through action and his need to tackle the larger moral issues of his time.

Victor McLaglen giving a superb study of Gypo in
THE INFORMER

3. Old Ireland: The Informer, The Rising of the Moon

Whitman once allegorised Ireland as "an ancient and sorrowful mother crouching over a grave . . . at her feet fallen an unused royal harp," an image with which Ford would sympathise. Devoted to Ireland, but more especially to Ireland's problems, he sees it as a country of immense honesty and humour whose generous capacity for living has been choked for centuries by attempts to impose foreign standards and rules of behaviour. Uncritically affectionate, Ford forgives in Ireland the excesses for which he condemns America; the puritanism of the Law and Order League that turns out the rotten elements in *Stagecoach* has its parallel in the formal traditions against which Sean Thornton fights for Mary Kate in *The Quiet Man*, but as Ford raises no voice against such repression when it has an Irish flavour, one senses that, to him, the worth of Irish rituals and institutions transcends their often inhumane application. His condemnation of the personal vices—greed, lust, pride—and his insistence on making all his films cautionary lessons has led him to accept and re-use frequently those typically Irish expressions of passion that, without transgressing the moral laws of community, allow pleasure and an outlet for animal spirits; the dance, the song, the fight and especially the drinking bout. There are no lechers in Ford's films, and few of the cardinal sins are represented in even his most unsympathetic characters, but pugnacity and drunkenness are regularly employed as symbols of pleasure and release, indissolubly linked with honesty, integrity and community spirit. Although, to Ford, the traits of "Irishness" can appear in any country or community, their most expressive symbol is the character of Victor McLaglen, a personification of noisy, violent, drunken but lovable Ireland, and based, Ford acknowledges, on his own father. No matter in what role he appears—Gypo in *The Informer,* Sergeants Mulcahy and Quincannon in *Fort Apache* and *She Wore a Yellow*

Ribbon respectively, "Red" Will Danaher in *The Quiet Man*—his insubordination and drunkenness remain constant, treated by Ford not as faults but as Irish virtues, consistent with conviviality and community feeling, just as Will's opposition to Sean's marriage to Mary Kate in *The Quiet Man* is acceptable because it stems from a respect for ritual.

Ford makes a point of introducing these apparent faults early in the story and quite arbitrarily, in scenes like Quincannon making his morning report to Brittles in *She Wore a Yellow Ribbon* and covertly helping himself to a swig from the captain's hidden bottle, or that in *Fort Apache*, where the three sergeants, ordered to destroy a stock of "bad" whisky, can only think of drinking it ("It's a man's task we have before us today," Mulcahy says in satisfied contemplation). Like the pugnacity of Quirt and Flagg or the financial dishonesty of Guthrie McCabe in *Two Rode Together* and Frank Skeffington in *The Last Hurrah*, drunkenness is no vice if indulged in for the sake of fellowship. It is only drinking without company that Ford finds reprehensible, since such an act, instead of contributing to community spirit, marks only a desire to escape from responsibility, a strong theme in Ford's remarkable first critical success, *The Informer* (1935).

Hailed on its release by the stuffier American critics, who decided that the film, with its overt symbolic language and lavish European surface, was one they could compare with the latest continental masterpieces, *The Informer*'s excessive reputation was rightly deflated in the late Forties. But in rejecting the extravagance of its style critics ignored the film's deep conviction, its assured technique, and McLaglen's superb study of the traitor Gypo which he was never to equal. Rambling through the fog-bound Dublin night, desperately demanding from society the love, security, eventually the forgiveness it is eager to give but which his sense of sacrifice prevents him from accepting, Gypo is a basic Ford character, responding neither to conventional rules of behaviour nor even to those of Liam O'Flaherty's story, but to the ingrained yet inexpressible need that dominates all Ford's heroes. Although Gypo's motives are characterised by the picture of an ocean liner and its promise of an American paradise, he is driven to betray his friend to the police less by the hope of escape than by a need to act against his society, to assert himself as an individual. He is unable to see that he is loved, that there is a place for him; like Ethan Edwards in *The Searchers* and Driscoll in *The Long Voyage Home*, moving on has become an end in itself, resisting authority a way of life.

In support of this, Ford shows Gypo wandering in a world for which he is too clumsy, too stupid, too large, and to which his needs and ideas are impossibly alien. Only the warm world of community offers him a hope of peace, but he flees from the light that beckons, creeps inside only to retreat once again into the fog at the first sign of friendship. He moves through a mist that is both physical and mental, bumping into people, striking his head on a sign, and his encounters with others, even at his trial, are marked by a total lack of communication. The ambiance and morality are uniquely Fordian. While it is not easy to separate the contribution of Dudley Nichols from that of Ford, the contrast between a pattern of visual symbolism that we know to be the scenarist's—the blind man who seems to pursue Gypo, the "Wanted" poster that blows after him, the phantom ghost of the murdered man—and some of the more significant detail of Gypo's performance suggest that, although much of the film is Nichols's, the underlying structure, as well as the ingenious use made of dialogue, is Ford's responsibility. (The script itself was a collaboration between Ford, Nichols and James K. McGuinness, and the gloomy camera style partly dictated by the low-budget necessities of shooting on small sets.) Ford's signature seems especially clear in the Catholic imagery of scenes such as that in which Katie (Margot Grahame) slips back her Madonna-like shawl to reveal the hard and over-painted face of a whore (a gesture repeated twenty years later in *The Fugitive*, Ford's most overtly Catholic work) and Gypo's final gesture of crucifixion as he dies begging forgiveness of his victim's mother in a church.

Equally typical of Ford, though less religiously oriented, is the beautiful scene where a street balladeer (Dennis O'Dea) sings "The Minstrel Boy" on a corner to his friend's scratchy violin. Two policemen come by, search the boy and then pass on, one pressing a coin into his raised hand. Revolving obediently as he is searched, the boy, without halting his song, comes full circle to his old position and, continuing the movement, tosses the tip contemptuously away. Such incidents, as well as showing Ford's deft touch with significant gesture, reflect his unashamedly melodramatic response to the Irish "Troubles" which, although he returned to them as a subject regularly throughout his career, either directly or with thinly disguised parallels like that in *The Grapes of Wrath*, he was never able to see in terms other than that of a sacred confrontation between regimented English brutality and Irish resolution, which the latter would always win. The third section of the unsatisfactory *The Rising of the Moon*, where two girls dressed as nuns rescue a condemned Irish patriot from jail under the noses of the law, is, not insignificantly, one of the few works in Ford's career that rivals in elaborate photographic style the excesses of *The Informer*, the entire twenty minute episode being shot with tilted camera, an extraordinary misuse of this conceit. Perhaps, to Ford, the "Troubles" were the world turned upside down, a time of dislocation and disorder that could be depicted only with the most bizarre style.

The Rising of the Moon (1957) was the bastard offspring of a long-standing love affair with the Irish film industry that seldom brought Ford more than disappointment. His projects for Irish production fell through or were long delayed; the most successful, *The Quiet Man*, was announced in 1937 as his first film for the ill-fated Renowned Artists company, but did not eventuate until 1952; a plan to film James Stevens's *The Demi-Gods* in Ireland after *The Quiet Man* never materialised; he was prevented from importing all the Abbey Theatre Players for *The Plough and the Stars* in 1936 and forced by pneumonia to discontinue his 1965 production of *Young Cassidy*. In addition, *The Rising of the Moon* was a commercial and artistic failure, though not without some incidental charm. Its faults are synopsised by the stiff introductory passage, where Tyrone Power, tweeds, house-front and brogue equally false, declares that his own Irish heritage, hitherto unsuspected by audiences, has led him to associate himself with "a couple of friends" to form Four Provinces Productions and make this film. Based on three short pieces, its wide variation in style and the often stifling "Irishness" of the plots, on whose simple structure Ford and scenarist Frank Nugent imposed layers of additional detail and incident, some superbly Fordian, the rest, like that added to Frank O'Connor's "The Majesty of the Law" quite extraneous, make *The Rising of the Moon* an irritating, though occasionally charming work.

O'Connor's original story, brief and told mainly in dialogue, showed the police sergeant coming to call on old Dan O'Flaherty, chatting with him for a few hours, then embarrassedly raising the subject of Dan's arrest for injuring another man in a fight. After establishing that Dan is not prepared, on principle, to pay the fine, a gentlemanly arrangement is made about his voluntary appearance at prison a few days hence and the sergeant leaves. Ford and Nugent expand on this with a typical inflation of detail, most of it consistent with Ford's attitudes. Dan (Noel Purcell) is no longer a solitary old man living as he had when his mother was alive, but the last of a noble line, his cottage built in the shadow of a ruined tower from whose stones it was constructed. Creeping around the ruin and maintaining his still in its base in Jack McGowran's impish bootlegger, supplying peat whisky to Dan and the friends who, answering Ford's need to emphasise drinking as a convivial community activity, turn up halfway through his conversation with the sergeant (Cyril Cusack). Later, as Dan is leaving for jail, the man he has injured arrives, flourishing the money for Dan's fine, but the old man, proudly refusing it, quietly says goodbye to his home and friends and, pausing only to pick up a stone, kiss it and put it into his pocket as a reminder, makes his way to prison.

That the additions are excessive need not be underlined; that they

53

are typical of Ford makes them more acceptable. His signature is in every incident, from the crude evocation of a reverence for the soil in Dan's self-conscious kissing of the stone through the private joke of mentioning one Sean O'Fienne—Ford's own Irish name—as having died and been buried recently down to the lonely tower and tiny cottage that to Ford symbolise Ireland's vanished glory as the film celebrates the durability of its social structure. *The Majesty of the Law* also casts an interesting light on Ford's attitude to money, which is as rigorous and consistent as his view on liquor. Both are acceptable as long as they are not an end in themselves. A cavalier disregard for money characterises many of Ford's heroes, often dramatised in the gesture of throwing down a bag of gold, while theft or the profitable exercise of capitalism are regarded with contempt; almost without exception, Ford's villains are businessmen. Dan O'Flaherty has money, and proudly exhumes his hoard from under the hearthstone to prove it, but cash comes a bad second to principle, as the shot of his victim (whom Ford makes a "gombeen man", ie. a money-lender) waving a handful of notes and promising forgiveness makes clear. Dan's rejection of the offer is no weakness, while the gombeen man lowers himself by thinking that money could influence the essential moral choice. It is typical of Ford that he regrets the scene in *The Quiet Man* where Mary Kate, after having at last extracted her dowry from the reluctant Will, should burn the money, and wish that, instead, he had had her give it to charity. To make the gesture *and* keep the money is hard-headedness combined with sentiment in the true Ford manner.

The middle episode of *The Rising of the Moon, One Minute Wait*, is a gem that deserves wider circulation than the two segments that support it. Adapted from a play by Michael J. McHugh, it is the liveliest of Irish humour, national without being parochial, handled with a perfect balance of wit and clever character observation. As a train's one minute wait at a country station becomes an hour to accommodate the late arrival of some lobsters for the Bishop's Golden Jubilee dinner, a pedigree goat on its way to a new owner, the

Cyril Cusack in THE RISING OF THE MOON

insistence of the driver on finishing the ghost story he is recounting to an awed barmaid (as well as his pint of beer), and finally the triumphant hurling team on its way back from the big match, the passengers calmly get on with their business, from arranging a marriage to, in the case of a stuffy English couple, trying vainly to get a cup of tea. The ensemble playing of Jimmy O'Dea as the porter, Tony Quinn as the station-master and J. G. Devlin as the guard is of the sort Ford uses admirably in the supporting casts of his features, full of marvellous expressions and gestures that could only be his invention. In this case the conflict revolves around the allegedly disreputable past of the guard, whose father, as the porter threatens to reveal should he not delay the train for the bishop's lobsters, "took to drink at eighty-six and died before his time," not to mention a sister "who went to America under very peculiar circumstances." The crowning revelation comes when he is prevented from abandoning the hurling team by a mention of his grandfather who was "seen in famine time creeping up an alley *with a bowl of soup*." The touch is light, but still we see the familiar Ford motifs; the drinking, a reverence, even in jest, for the historical past and the church, an affirmation of community rituals—the bishop's anniversary, the story, the game—that transcends the railway timetable.

Relentless use of the tilted camera mars the third section, *1921*, but Ford's observation of an ingenious plan to rescue condemned Irish patriot Sean Curran (Donal Donnelly) from jail is direct enough to overshadow, though not obliterate altogether, the obtrusive style, heavily symbolic settings and lack of a central character. The story, nevertheless, sounds true, though none of it appeared in Lady Gregory's original play: two girls dressed as nuns enter the jail, one pretending to be the condemned man's sister. Bluffing the British officer in charge, they are left alone with Curran, then ushered out just before the appointed time of execution. But the guards find, on coming for the man, that he has been replaced by one of the girls, whose American passport guarantees immunity from prosecution. Meanwhile, Curran hides out in a small theatre, where he is dressed as an extra in what appears to be a stolid performance of *Riders to the Sea*. Still in the same disguise, accompanied by a donkey and a basket of sheet music, he passes himself off as Jimmy Walsh, the ballad singer, bluffs his way past the police and is rowed out to a waiting ship, watched by the policeman (Dennis O'Dea) who has been half aware throughout of the plot, but influenced not to reveal it by the galling authority of the "Black and Tans."

This is one of the few examples of a Ford character altering noticeably during the course of a story. After obediently controlling the crowd of silent observers outside the jail, the policeman has a brief argument with a British officer and then, almost imperceptibly, discards his stolid immobility and mutters "Move along, there: keep moving," for the motion of the crowd, whose shuffling parade he joins. The only person to suspect the nuns' disguise, he is also on duty at the spot where Curran meets the escape boat, but lets the man go after an ambiguous conversation about a song. "I used to sing it myself," he says reflectively, "though there was a bit of treason in it. But there's a bit of treason in us all." In fact there is as much treason in the song as the man, and the choice of Curran's disguise as a ballad singer seems especially appropriate, associating the fugitive with the song, to Ford a powerful affirmation of ritual and historical tradition, and thus setting him high in the hierarchy of favourable characters. It hints also that what Ford finds most admirable in the Irish are pugnacity, insolence and devotion to community, traits that survive, like the treason in the song, even outside the borders of the country. In all his films, his response to the Irish landscape, a commonplace source of romance in most films on Ireland, is disinterest; except for some brief and attractive shots at the opening of *The Quiet Man* it is hardly seen, Ford preferring to concentrate his conflicts indoors, and his attention on the resilience of the Irish. If one spirit can be said to distinguish the three major factors in Ford's personality—Catholicism, militarism, Irishness—it is that of durability, the will and ability to survive and prevail despite overwhelming contrary pressures. Ford's church is eternal, his army unconquerable, his Irish men indestructible, and the concept of force, moral or physical, applied either by individuals or groups, is central to all his films.

Victor McLaglen, Katharine Hepburn, and John Ford on the set of
MARY OF SCOTLAND

4. Going Home Again: Mary of Scotland, The Fugitive

As echoes of the Holy Family, the Trinity and the eternal Church enrich many of Ford's most moving films, so subsidiary Catholic themes like the parable of the Prodigal Son distinguish his more personal works, those films that, over the years, he has chosen as his favourites. Many share the theme of a man who breaks away from his community and beliefs, experiences a crisis of faith, returns to the fold and is welcomed back. That the community and beliefs are often spiritual, and the welcome death is immaterial, since it is made clear throughout Ford's films that a death for one's principles guarantees immortality. The theme is explored in *Young Mr. Lincoln* and *The Informer*, and referred to often in *The Sun Shines Bright*, which is dominated by the concept of forgiveness and redemption; the film opens with a trial at which a young Negro is acquitted after the judge has been influenced by a song (the ubiquitous "Dixie") to forgive his offence. Later, the immoral Ashby Corwin (John Russell) is moved to repent at a funeral, falling on his knees to recite the only prayer he knows, a child's "Gentle Jesus, Meek and Mild," while the dying prostitute (Dorothy Jordan) redeems herself by returning home to be reunited with her daughter. This key theme, and the larger issue of martyrdom for a cause, is examined most ambitiously in two of Ford's least seen and discussed films, *Mary of Scotland* (1936) and *The Fugitive* (1947).

Separated in setting and historical background, related by source only insofar as both come from distinguished literary originals, *Mary of Scotland* from Maxwell Anderson's austere verse play, *The Fugitive* from Graham Greene's novel *The Power and the Glory*, and in approach only in that Dudley Nichols is responsible for both scripts, these films, superficially, differ to a degree that makes them irreconcilable. Even their production histories are almost comically varied; *The Fugitive* is an American adaptation of an English novel shot in Mexico, while *Mary of Scotland* is Hollywood's version of a

59

Scottish event with a cast containing countless English *émigrés*. Nevertheless, Ford's vision unites them, making each film a work of arresting if occasionally obscure quality, deserving closer attention. Only Ford, who likes both, seems to have any genuine appreciation of their merit.

Each begins, as do many other Ford works, with the main character emerging from the background, isolated and alone. In *Mary of Scotland* a ship looms out of the fog bringing Mary (Katharine Hepburn) from France to make her doomed bid for the English throne, while in *The Fugitive*, Henry Fonda's hunted priest, whose story, Ford stresses in a spoken introduction, is "as old as the Bible," underlining the Prodigal aspect, walks calmly along an arched collonade and into the countryside, passing through sleeping villages to reach his dark and deserted church. And both films end with the same symbol of resurrection; as Mary mounts the scaffold, the camera tilts off her exalted face to the stormy sky and the thunder of her lover's pipers while, as the priest dies in front of a firing squad, his wooden cross in his hand as Mary's gold one gleams on her breast, the fact of his assumption into heaven is conveyed by the same shots of the sky and the action of his killer crossing himself in an image of absolution. Between these two moments, both have fought a losing battle with their destinies, resisting the pain and death they know has been prepared for them, but succumbing finally to the moral necessity of fate. In fighting to stay alive, they sacrifice their integrity, Mary to her love for Bothwell (Fredric March), and the promise of escape, the priest to a fear of death that, to the disgust of contemporary critics, replaced the alcoholism with which it was represented in Greene's book. It need not be repeated that Ford cannot see drunkenness as a vice, and his sole gesture in this direction in *The Fugitive*, where the priest tries to buy wine for a mass, is largely unsuccessful and not without comic elements. But as cowardice is a recognisable fault, tinged with a threat to solidarity and group effort, Ford's evocation of the priest's fear as he moves desperately through the countryside pursued by his guilt in the form of J. Carroll Naish's

Mary (Katharine Hepburn) on the staircase in MARY OF SCOTLAND

wheedling informer, is among the film's most powerful elements. Queen Mary's weakness is linked with her human failings, her femininity, not with her Catholicism, as the priest's is linked with his fear, not his beliefs, which in both cases become the only force by which the heroes can be sustained in their hour of trial. Figures who have represented the lure of escape—the spy, Mary's lover— suffer or die in degradation while the heroes who have kept faith go to glory as the belief that sustains them moves inexorably on.

A costume picture, *Mary of Scotland* offers less opportunity for the gestures and symbols on which Ford depends for dramatic emphasis, although he is assisted by Nichols's reasonably faithful adaptation of the Anderson play; little of the poetic dialogue is left, and some of the incidents, like Mary's affair with Bothwell, have been softened and sentimentalised, but most of the play's important set-pieces remain, such as the final (fictitious) meeting between Elizabeth and Mary that clarifies the central issue and allows Mary, confident that her son will inherit the throne she was denied, to go calmly to the block. Even the most lifeless aspects of these confrontations and the self-conscious dialogue are handled by Ford with assurance. Refusing to be overawed by the extravagant sets, he makes full use of them, setting Mary in low angle against elaborately-painted ceilings and heavy staircases to show her dominated but not defeated by the burdens of her historical role, a style that reaches its peak in the trial scene, where the lone woman faces five implacable judges who glare down at her from their dais. Ford's mastery of this and other sets, his ability to give furniture a meaning, is perfectly displayed in both *Mary of Scotland* and *The Fugitive*, the trial scene of the first having its parallel in the early church sequence of the second. Mary, resisting the judges' charge that she connived at treason against Elizabeth, demands to be faced by her accuser, but is told that the queen is present "symbolically" in the form of an empty throne on which lie the emblems of royalty—sceptre, orb and crown. She is invited to sit down rather than remain standing, a gesture that would reduce her to parity with Elizabeth's regalia, empty symbol rather than person. "I prefer to stand," she says with irony, "symbolically," and does so until the death of Bothwell is announced. Then, wearily, she slumps in the chair, human weakness betraying the higher purpose, a sin of which she does not absolve herself until her last prayer in the cell before execution.

In *The Fugitive*, Ford's handling of a similar sequence of events is more hieratic, though no less compelling. The priest stands alone in his old church, its images smashed by the persecutors, its font overturned, even its cross torn down. As he throws open the doors, his shadow in the moonlight streams into the church, his outstretched arms making him into a personalisation of the cross, showing both that the priest is marked for sacrifice, that the cross is, in a sense, in

Henry Fonda, silhouetted against the light, confronts Dolores del Rio in church during THE FUGITIVE

him, and that therefore he embodies his belief as Mary does hers. He resists, as she does, the opposing symbolism, in her case Elizabeth's regalia, for him the smashed church, and celebrates it, as Mary did, in a gesture of defiance; she stands when told to sit, declines to sign a confession in return for life; he blesses the peasants and baptises the bastard child of the woman (Dolores del Rio) who befriends him. It is easy to criticise the pictorial extravagance of these scenes in *The Fugitive*, with their streaming shadows, overt religious images like the re-erection of the font, the procession of singing peasants, the figure of del Rio, draped like the madonna and carrying a child, equally to wince at Richard Hageman's syrupy and oppressive score, but less so to ignore the conviction with which Ford invests them, the unmistakable piety of his approach with its emphasis on the significant trivia of Catholic ritual; the holy water, the candles, the bell he tolls to call the townspeople to church. The sense of a community returning with gratitude and pleasure to shared rituals is both Fordian and human, as much a catharsis as any dance or fight in his more localised American films.

The priest's self-betrayal also has the quiet poignance of Mary's slow collapse into the fatal chair, the same assured contrast between

The procession from THE FUGITIVE

visual drama and private despair. Pedro Armendariz's police lieutenant rears his horse before the assembled peasants and demands they give up the priest who is hiding in disguise among them, drags off the village head man as a hostage and, when the priest half-heartedly protests (though retaining his incognito), asks whether he wishes to take the chief's place and when the offer is refused, contemptuously dismisses him as "not much of a man."

Deaths in both films are given a powerfully heightened significance; David Rizzio, Mary's confidant and secretary, elegantly played by John Carradine, scampers in horror from room to room as the swordsmen pursue him, then falls to the bed and draws a coverlet across his face so as not to see the dagger slicing into his body; Bothwell, alone and sick in a foreign prison, has a vision of Mary and dies in a windstorm that symbolises his mental turmoil. In *The Fugitive*, Ward Bond's Calvert, the American thief who alone understands the priest, dies helping him, harassing a troop of mounted police in a night battle among jagged stalks of corn, after his essential similarity to the priest—both are men of force and honour, though in the spiritual and temporal worlds respectively—has been symbolised by a shot of them passing in the fields, the screen divided mathematically by a low stone wall, one man walking towards the camera, the other away from it. Faced with Ford's sketch of the thief who alone has faith in the ideals of the fugitive holy man, one thinks automatically of Dismas and "Today thou shalt be with me in Paradise," one of many parallels with the agony and death of Christ that appear in this film.

As in most of Ford's work, contrasts and conflicts of opposed personalities provide motivation for the action, the rival parties not meeting until the end of the story, an event that in both cases comes just before death. And again in keeping with Ford's usual attitude, the forces in each film that oppose the hero are not villainous, but justifiable causes held by people hardly less sincere than those whom they assault. Their integrity is unmistakable. Elizabeth opposes Mary not out of malice but because to leave her alive is to nurture a

65

threat to her country's security, while Armendariz's police officer genuinely hates and despises the reactionary corruption with which he associates the church, but which is more aptly symbolised by police superintendent Leo Carrillo, who secretly accepts bribes and trades in liquor while professing to support the new morality. The instant when the lieutenant kicks aside his chief's hat-box with its new Panama in order to polish his high military boots is one of Ford's ingenious encapsulations in gesture of this antipathy. Elizabeth's court, efficient and formal, in contrast to Mary's, where baying dogs compete for attention with the brawling council and John Knox can burst in with his congregation to call down hellfire on the Papist queen, is emblematic of her character as Mary's of hers; so, in *The Fugitive*, the lieutenant's well-drilled troop of mounted police contrasts with the squalor surrounding the superintendent and his cousin's bar where liquor is sold illegally and to which the priest is lured for a comic drinking bout in his search for wine to say a mass. But since the virtue of Elizabeth and Mary, the lieutenant and the priest is identical, Ford draws the necessary dramatic distinction between them by attributing to the characters of Elizabeth and the lieutenant a fatal lapse into self-interest that gives to their adversaries the final moral triumph. Mary and the priest win their fights by remaining faithful to their principles, despite earlier defection, but at the climax Elizabeth and the lieutenant weaken, the queen by personally confronting her cousin as she has declined to do through-out the story (and in real life never did), the lieutenant by making a superstitious sign of the cross as the priest dies. In each case, the gesture of weakness can be traced back to an act of selfishness of which they have not repented, in the case of childless Elizabeth the wish to revenge herself on Mary and her son, and in that of the lieutenant his seduction and abandonment of the peasant girl whose child the priest christens in the opening sequence. Mary, concerned only for her rights and her faith, and the priest, uninterested in the girl and devoted to his beliefs, both prevail, while their assailants, like the self-interested in all Ford films, fall and are left desolate.

Mary of Scotland, though superbly engineered by Ford and his collaborators, is essentially a studio production in which Ford's usual imagery has insufficient room to expand, but *The Fugitive*, by contrast, is one of his most personal and deeply significant works, its examination of religious conscience making it fit to be compared with the greatest European films on this theme. Far from being the "dishonest" work of *Sequence*'s estimation, *The Fugitive* if often painfully frank and open in its dealing with a subject obviously close to Ford's emotions; its faults, and one does not deny their existence, stem from the director's characteristic inability to function as a detached stylist when his feelings are engaged. The use of Ford's language of religious symbolism is, one admits, often too obvious for true stylistic balance; contrasts between characters are drawn on many occasions with a lack of subtlety that reduces some scenes to a grotesque level of melodrama, and Fonda lacks the detail in his character that might have made him less a symbol and more a man. But if one balances against these the richness of the conception, the depth of feeling in almost every gesture and scene, the insight Ford so clearly conveys into the nature of belief and the higher motivations of spirituality, they seem minor, ruffles on the surface of an otherwise smooth and confident work.

The lonely passenger (Dorothy Jordan) on the jetty of THE SUN SHINES BRIGHT as the steamboat disappears into the distance

5. In Monument Valley: Stagecoach, Fort Apache, She Wore a Yellow Ribbon

"I feel that Nature is played out as a Beauty," Thomas Hardy wrote, "but not as a Mystery. I don't want to see landscapes. I want to see the deeper reality underlying the scenic, the expression of what are sometimes called abstract imaginings." Ford, one feels, would have an automatic sympathy with Hardy's need to give conventional scenic backgrounds an emotional power and significance, since it is in keeping with his overall tendency to assign objects and gestures an emotional truth in addition to their ordinary story-telling value. Even in Ford's early Westerns, one senses a special significance in the shapes and shades of the American landscape, though the use he made of them was relatively crude. *Three Bad Men*, for instance, has none of the consistency in the use of plain and mountains that distinguishes *Fort Apache*, and the riverside landscape of *Cameo Kirby*, later used with emotional effect in *The Sun Shines Bright* with shots like that of the departing steamboat, and its lonely passenger, the dying prostitute, isolated on the wharf against the sickly sun, lacks any such acid poignancy. Ford was, one feels, waiting for a location that would allow him to make his most important synthesis of moral and dramatic statement.

That Ford regards landscape as of vital symbolic importance becomes increasingly apparent in his Thirties films, where this interest in natural features develops in conjunction with a sophistication in the use of objects and gestures to give his films a subliminal undercurrent. Shots like that of the terrified Darnley in *Mary of Scotland* staring at the knife which glows supernaturally as he realises he must kill with it are quite beyond the Ford of the silent period, showing a precise yet highly complex sense of the value even the simplest object can have. After *The Informer* and his collaboration with Dudley Nichols, Ford linked natural features in his outdoor films with social or personal situations; a hill, difficult to climb, became in *How Green Was My Valley* a representation of less

69

palpable problems. Rivers come to represent rest, peace, the elegant ease of aristocratic life; Cameo Kirby and Dr. John Pearly in *Steamboat round the Bend* each travel the Mississippi in palatial steamboats, while in *Four Men and a Prayer* a vital clue to the gun-runners is revealed on a river cruise as Loretta Young in an evening gown is framed against the fan-tail and white wake; in *Two Rode Together*. Guthrie McCabe and Jim Gary rest by the river, and in *The Grapes of Wrath* it is an almost Biblical symbol of relaxation and cleansing. By contrast, islands are associated with detachment from society and thus with despair; in Ford's "island" pictures, the heroes—Terangi in *The Hurricane*, Dr. Mudd in *The Prisoner of Shark Island*, the Navy men of *They Were Expendable*, the hedonistic "Guns" and "Boats" of *Donovan's Reef*—fight a fatal isolation from their communities with growing mental and emotional strain, a conflict most often relieved by a storm that represents final psychological release. But nowhere is this conjunction of landscape and attitude more apparent than in Ford's films shot on his favourite location, Monument Valley.

That this extraordinary area, an ancient sea-floor with sandstone massifs jutting out of a red and featureless plain, the cliffs worn into soaring pinnacles by centuries of weathering, was chosen by Ford as the setting for his most famous films confirms the conviction that its landscape is central to Ford's view of the world. Like Yellowstone, where *North of Hudson Bay,* and parts of *The Searchers* and *Cheyenne Autumn* were shot, it is an area with little relation to the conventional geography of the West, a patchwork of natural features lending itself to subjective interpretation. To Ford, Monument Valley was appealing precisely because its features were sufficiently unusual to be free of conventional emotional associations; its plains and pinnacles did not share a generally agreed symbolic meaning as does a mountain range or a field of wheat, and they could therefore be used as Ford used more easily manipulated natural phenomena like wind or light, as symbols of a particular morality, a view of the world that would be reflected in the world itself. Ford's style is perfectly mirrored in this

Coach and escort ride across the panorama of Monument Valley during STAGECOACH

landscape, the measured flow of his theme in the flat plain, its dramatic peaks in the sudden eruptions of stone around which he always sets his major battles and dramatic confrontations, while his concept of society, in which man, orderly and respectful of rules, maintains the natural order in the shadow of unassailable principles, seems emblematised in his films of the cavalry fighting and dying among the valley's stones while overhead the omnipresent clouds suggest a higher reality of mind and of the spirit to which all are subservient.

Like the land, which is stripped of all excess, reduced to bare geological bones, Ford's films in this setting deal most intimately with the realities of the Fordian universe; duty, death, example. Man and earth interpenetrate in these dramas to an extent not found in the rest of his work. In *The Grapes of Wrath* and *The Rising of the Moon* the soil and its influence are noted, but *The Searchers, Fort Apache* and *She Wore a Yellow Ribbon* postulate a far more mysterious relationship; we become aware of landscape as a factor in life, affecting, one sometimes feels almost controlling the fate of those isolated here. In all the Monument Valley films, the ability to read the signs of the land—dust, weather, smoke—and use them to advantage is assigned by Ford as a strong indication of worth, or at the very least, of power. Dust in particular begins to have great importance; in *Fort Apache, Cheyenne Autumn* and *She Wore a Yellow Ribbon* it is both an omen and a component of fate, used to warn and to deceive; in *Fort Apache* it is an aspect of landscape as important as hill or cliff. When a group of soldiers chased by Indians leads the pursuers into a larger troop that has been following for this purpose, Ford, with a perfectly-used high shot, shows the rescuers racing past and below the camera into the fight, throwing up a cloud of dust from which the fleeing troop and its wagon emerge, the action obscured in dust behind them. This is not only a shrewdly-realised *coup de théâtre* but one that reduces the issue to the constituent elements of Man and Earth; the Indians' revolt is not against the cavalry but against the natural order which the valley symbolises and the cavalry guards. The Indian chief's gesture before the final battle of letting a handful of earth trickle through his fingers is a symbolic expression of his mastery of the land, a dominance Thursday has forfeited by his dishonourable conduct and which only the campaigns of *She Wore a Yellow Ribbon,* where the landscape again assumes its rightful importance in man's life, can retrieve for the cavalry. Thursday's decision to charge at the dust cloud the Indians raise as a diversion and lure in the final battle suggests the Nature against which he has set himself, the landscape mirroring exactly the resistance to cavalry traditions that causes his downfall. The concept of Man as *of* the earth is not original with Ford, but derived by him from the literal creation of Adam from earth in Genesis, an aspect of the symbol Ford uses often; in *The Searchers* a hunting party finds under a stone the corpse of a dead Indian, the dusty body, in paint and feathers, set in its shallow grave implying a ritual return to earth that Ford dwells on often in his countless funeral scenes, while both *The Grapes of Wrath* and *How the West Was Won* have burial sequences where the grave-diggers are enveloped in dust which Ford carefully back-lights in a precise visual reference to the Biblical "And unto dust thou shalt return."

Fort Apache makes impressive use of Monument Valley, almost

Soldiers digging graves from HOW THE WEST WAS WON

every action being dictated by its features, although the essential dramatic conflict is ethical. At the centre of the story are two opposites, Colonel Owen Thursday (Henry Fonda) and Captain Kirby York (John Wayne), though their differences are a matter of politics and honour as well as personality. Frank Nugent's script makes Thursday from the North, York from the South; Thursday arrogant, York proud; Thursday's temper slow, York's quick; Thursday formal, York easy; Thursday a textbook general, York an intuitive skirmisher. York is the cavalry, Thursday the independent individual who dislikes the rules of ritual (perfectly conveyed when Thursday, with obvious reluctance, fulfils his duty in dancing with the Sergeant-Major's wife at the Non-Commissioned Officers' Ball and leading the Grand March) and is at last destroyed by his contempt for them, seduced by his own pride and the prospect of a prestigious victory into a textbook action against a band of fugitive Apaches that ends in a massacre. Like many of Ford's films, *Fort Apache* is closely related to a second work whose theme and approach it shares, in this case *She Wore a Yellow Ribbon,* Ford's second classic cavalry film and one which explores the theme with a skill that *Rio Grande*, the third segment of the so-called "Cavalry Trilogy," does not share. In *She Wore a Yellow Ribbon*, the emphasis is not on the defiance of ritual as in *Fort Apache* but on Captain Nathan Brittles's championship and affirmation of it. It is his judgement of the Indian campaign that triumphs, and when he goes out to affirm his principles as Thursday in his futile charge affirmed his, it is in response to the unwritten duty of a commander to honour his promise, a gesture that, unlike Thursday's, is met with success and honourable retirement as Head of Scouts. Woven into both films is the same subsidiary romance of a young lieutenant (John Agar in both cases) and the commander's daughter, the comic relief of the inevitable Irish non-commissioned officers, led by Victor McLaglen, the motifs of family life, of parental authority vs. individuality, and of the triumphant North gingerly integrating with the unreconstructed South that are common to most of Ford's films with Nugent.

74

John Wayne and Ben Johnson in the burial scene from SHE WORE A YELLOW RIBBON

But the easy analysis of themes and plots evades us, since *Fort Apache* and *She Wore a Yellow Ribbon* differ vastly in mood, while both are separate from Ford's other cavalry films in Monument Valley, *Rio Grande* and *Sergeant Rutledge*. In theme and pictorial style *She Wore a Yellow Ribbon* is a film of twilight. Ford asked his cameraman to re-create the mood of frontier artist Frederick Remington, and Winton Hoch, whose photography won an Oscar, obliged with slanting sunlight that echoes the haunting melancholy of Remington's more personal works, a mood reflected in the tired and undramatic shooting. One is struck by how little riding there is in *She Wore a Yellow Ribbon*, how courageously Ford discards the glamour of the "pony soldiers" to suggest instead their human weakness. The film's most moving scenes relate vitally to the nature of the ground, and by implication to the moral significance of the valley. Brittles, whether alone in the graveyard talking to his dead wife or crouched by the dying "Trooper Smith" (a Brigadier General of the Confederacy who enlisted in the Northern ranks) and officiating later at his funeral, seems inhabited by the spirit of the earth, an expression of its stern morality. Reflecting this, other related scenes— the report of the wounded trooper in which he respectfully taxes Brittles with his non-appearance at the appointed relief station, the operation on this trooper conducted on a jolting wagon as the group leads its horses through a rumbling storm, the exchanges between the lovers Olivia Pennell and Flint Cohill—are set not on horseback but on the ground, Ford adopting an intimate style of medium shots to emphasise the vulnerability of these men and at the same time their affinity with the landscape.

She Wore a Yellow Ribbon is a film of force against the individual, of a single rider pursued by dozens of attackers, of one man accepting the burden of command, of personal honour, of the cavalry society severely tested. Its tone is set by the opening shot of pennants fallen and dishonoured at the Little Big Horn, the spoken introduction, "Custer is dead and around the bloody guidons of the Seventh Cavalry lie the two hundred and twelve officers and men he led . . ." evoking the tragedy of Custer in the shadow of which the whole film lies. By contrast, *Fort Apache* is redolent of earlier times, a film where wounds like the Civil War still smart, where Northern pragmatism and Southern gallantry have not yet meshed, where a man like the Indian chief Geronimo, later (historically) to provide the menace in *Stagecoach* can be introduced casually as part of an Indian parley deputation with no suggestion of his future notoriety. The light is hard, the black-and-white photography factually sharp, the heroics and humour of cavalry warfare dwelt on in detail, and while in a thematic sense the film is about the anachronism of conventional fighting tactics, and as such relates to *She Wore a Yellow Ribbon* in that the destruction of Thursday will result in the diffuse and casual campaign of that film, its dramatic intent is to condemn not the methods of Thursday but the arrogance and individual pride that led to them being employed at the expense of his command. No bloody defeat colours this film as the Little Big Horn does *She Wore a Yellow Ribbon*; the comedy is robust, the songs lusty, the action exciting and heroic to a degree rare in Ford's films. It is a film of grand gestures in which both Thursday and York participate; York's angry response to Thursday's accusation of cowardice, a gauntlet thrown down and a challenge issued, is no different in form to Thursday's contemptuous council with the Indian leaders, in which he finds them "without honour," a charge answered by the extinction of his command, but once again Ford assigns varying emotional and dramatic values to the gestures with a use of his symbolically-charged landscape and a subtle variation in approach. York's challenge is personal, man against man, and couched in a ritual form honoured by long observance, Thursday's sweeping, careless of form—he cuts short Beaufort's courtly Spanish introductions and translations, demands instead an insulting brevity— and moved not by duty but by a wish to be famous. Suggesting this, York's gesture is shot against the neutral background of a ravine wall, the parley before a towering monolith that suggests the enormous truth against which Thursday sets himself. In the end, he is defeated less by the Indians than by his refusal to accept the truths of ritual, morality and landscape, charging his men into a box canyon filled with riflemen just as his policy has sent him riding recklessly against an unbreakable moral precept, the respect for community and mutually agreed rules of behaviour.

The ending of *Fort Apache* is one of the most difficult to interpret in all Ford's work. Entertaining a group of newsmen assigned to cover his campaign against the Indians, York, the new commander, discusses with them the now-famous Thursday's Charge. A reporter describes a painting of the event hanging in the White House, rhapsodising about "the Indians in their paint and feathered bonnets," a clear reference to John Mulvaney's "Custer's Last Rally" which Whitman saw in 1881 and described in almost identical terms. He suggests that it must have been a privilege to know Thursday. "No man died more bravely," York acknowledges ambiguously, "nor brought more honour to his regiment." As a second reporter recalls the other men who died in the charge, York, seeing their silhouetted shadows riding by outside, "The Battle Hymn of the Republic" accompanying them, says "They aren't forgotten because they aren't dead," and goes on to praise the selfless spirit of the soldiers who, despite poor pay, bad conditions and the expectation of an early and painful death, still do their duty. Then, putting on a cap which, like his newly spruce uniform, echoes Thursday's meticulous appearance, he leads the men out on patrol. The *volte face* seems irreconcilable with York's enmity and Thursday's errors, until we reassess an earlier scene in which York returns to rescue the wounded and unhorsed Thursday, only to have his help rejected, the colonel rejoining his men and dying with them. In this act, Thursday renounces personal ambition, reaffirming his essential nature as an honourable commander and absolving himself of his guilt for earlier blunders, as well as the abrogation of his responsibilities so superbly suggested by Ford with the image of Thursday's riderless horse leading the men into battle. Now a hero, Thursday may be honoured, imitated and aspired to as an ideal, but *Fort Apache* underlines how little society understands the real man or his motives, and how much the importance of heroes depends on the lessons others read into their lives, and deaths.

Rio Grande, a minor work (though not without value), has little in common with the first two cavalry films, showing a curious bitterness in Ford's story of an Army officer's divided family making painful attempts to re-integrate itself. The theme is individuality, independent action—John Wayne, again playing Kirby York, a lieutenant at a point in his career preceding *She Wore a Yellow Ribbon*, leads a secret mission into Mexico to destroy an Apache band—and many of the details have an exhibitionist quality alien to Ford, best dramatised in the horse-riding demonstration a trooper gives to York and the blatant featuring of "The Sons of the Pioneers," a vocal group best known for its appearance in Roy Rogers Westerns, as unlikely cavalrymen in order to insert a number of songs. The "trilogy" label has little justification. Ford made a number of films in which the Seventh Cavalry features, including *Cheyenne Autumn* and *Sergeant Rutledge*, but since the essential links in Ford's films are moral and emotional rather than thematic, the subject of all these films is seldom the cavalry but rather the order of community life placed in conflict with an opposing destructive force. Unlike *Rio Grande*, *Fort Apache* and *She Wore a Yellow Ribbon* are less military films than comments on civilisation and its impact on the frontier, each exploring one step in the civilising process. In *Fort Apache* the assumption that purely military ethics can sustain a community is challenged and proved wrong in an event clearly suggested by the Custer massacre which historically was a turning point in Western development, concentrating national attention on the area and its problems. Continuing the argument, *She Wore a Yellow Ribbon* dramatises the fact that private responsibility to universal standards of community must transcend arbitrary military rules, and in the romance of Olivia and Flint suggests that the next generation, while honouring the men who uphold them, may discard entirely the beliefs by which their elders lived. Characterisation and action support the thesis in both films. The people of *Fort Apache* are ambitious, on their way up; the recruits become troopers, the sergeant's son a lieutenant, the captain a colonel, but in *She Wore a Yellow Ribbon* the brightness of ambition has faded as the relevance of the cavalry declines. Both Brittles and Quincannon are in their last weeks before retirement, and the shadows of encroaching urban values, suggested in *Fort Apache* by the newspapermen and in both films by the crooked "sutlers" whose capitalism destroys the balance of power on which the cavalry depends, gather mournfully around the ageing Brittles.

For this reason, it's interesting, if one must have a trilogy, to count as its third part Ford's earlier *Stagecoach*, (1939) whose relationships to the cavalry films extend beyond the common Monument Valley setting to characters, themes and style. *Stagecoach* shows the end result of Western urbanisation, a town and its new values threatening to destroy the loose-knit but homogenous frontier community, with its intricate checks and balances of force and its reliance on individual honour. The frontier has its representative in Ringo (John Wayne) whose role relates closely to the John Agar, Ben Johnson and Jeffrey Hunter parts in later films, a young man whose lack of sophistication is balanced by a sense of honour, a devotion to community and an instinctive understanding of landscape and omens. On the coach journey which is the focus of this civilisation-frontier conflict, Ringo has on his side the honest professional law-man Curly (George Bancroft), who is taking him in to be tried for killing a man who helped to murder Ringo's brother. Among the passengers on the coach, most of whom have been ejected from a town that has developed a puritan morality during its brief life, he is opposed by the gentleman gambler Hatfield (John Carradine), a nervous whisky salesman (Donald Meek), Lucy Mallory, the pregnant wife of a cavalry officer (Louise Platt) to whom Hatfield attaches himself as a protector, and Gatewood (Berton Churchill), a defaulting bank manager with the town's savings in his bag. Instinctively, however, Ringo trusts the drunken Doc Boone (Thomas Mitchell) and falls in love with the prostitute Dallas (Claire Trevor) in whom he can see no fault.

Ford uses his method of identifying unpleasant social forces with unsympathetic individuals. Gatewood, Hatfield and Mrs. Mallory, uniting in contempt of Dallas and Doc Boone, render themselves, and thus by implication the urban values they hold, totally repellent. Ringo, on the other hand, becomes, in his simple devotion to the girl and his fixed intention to revenge the murder of his brother, the film's most sympathetic character, and his values assume an automatic glamour. The "town" characters are associated throughout with self-seeking and a lack of community spirit, to Ford twin aspects of capitalism; Gatewood's theft, significantly of community funds, Hatfield's lack of affiliation (he has even discarded his real name, though his devotion to family reappears at his death when he asks that his father be informed) and Lucy's refusal of help and comfort from Dallas and Boone during the uncomfortable coach journey are emblematic of city life and its rejection of true values. Ford's exploration of the tensions in this group is ingeniously accurate, carried on, as usual, in patterns of gestures and actions rather than words. The pointed contempt of Hatfield and Mrs. Mallory who ostentatiously leave the table where Dallas eats is answered by Ringo's simple gallantry in refusing to consider her as anything less than a lady, though Ford makes his courtliness too gauche; Ringo is surely no less adept than the others at recognising a whore when he sees one. Gatewood's capitalism and self-interest is underlined by his nervous clinging to the bag in which the loot is hidden, and in his protestations of dubious political principles; the country, he believes, would function well only in the hands of a president who is also a businessman, a view Ford the Republican finds unpleasant.

But the emotional conflicts of *Stagecoach*, like those of *Fort Apache* and *She Wore a Yellow Ribbon*, are finally clarified and resolved in terms of landscape rather than on the level of personality. When the coach arrives at the edge of the valley floor and the Indian attack begins, the issue becomes the common Fordian one of force against force, Ford discarding even conventional rules of editing to capture the vital individual shots of these opposing forces in action. The by-now conventional fast tracking shot where he follows a rider or vehicle at a dead run across the flat plain of the valley is more than a visual signature and homage to Remington; it conveys something essential in Ford's view of conflict. Beyond the cliffs and mesas with their suggestion of unassailable moral precepts, the issues are resolved into naked contests of strength, speed and endurance. The climactic flight in *Stagecoach* was one of Ford's first uses of the idea, but it recurs frequently in later Monument Valley films, chase occurring not among the hills but out on the featureless plain where no lesser issues intervene. (It is remarkable how much impact and meaning was lost when Gordon Douglas's Sixties re-make of *Stagecoach* transferred its location to the more conventional mountain landscape.) The meaning Ford attributes to even this simple visual device enriches minor shots like that in *Sergeant Rutledge*, where the Negro trooper wounded by an Indian lance is followed in the same flat tracking movement as he reels in the saddle, the normal contest of speed replaced by one between man and gravity.

A secondary aspect of these three films deserving closer consideration is Ford's attitude to the Indians, who throughout his Westerns provide a frequent vital plot element. To be consistent with his image of warm and lovable poet of the West, Ford's attitude to the Indians should be an affectionate and understanding response to them as human beings, but although his personal generosity to them is well known, he characterises them in most of his films as supernatural savages, brutal, sadistic, as much devils as men. Only *Cheyenne Autumn* makes an attempt to show Indians as individuals, but, like *Sergeant Rutledge* and that film's simplistic view of Negro emancipation, it is a case of too little too late, a move by Ford, perhaps commercially forced, to accommodate the changing views of the time. In both cases, his characterisation of the Negro and the Indian rings false; as his Mongolian warlord in *Seven Women* harks back to Thirties traditions of Indian Mutiny films, so Rutledge and his men and the Indians of *Cheyenne Autumn* are pasteboard copies of other models, or black characters who express essentially white Catholic values. Between the cringing Stepin' Fetchit of *The Sun Shines Bright* and the statuesquely posed Rutledge there is a difference only of style.

Although Ford's attitude to the Indians and the Negro is characteristic of his aristocratic sense of social inequality, it runs precisely counter to accepted patterns in American art, another proof of Ford's unique position as an individual artist. As Leslie Fiedler points out in *The Return of the Vanishing American*, literature most often saw the American West as "an unhumanised vastness" and the Indian as a symbol of new emotional and religious values, to whom the white man attracted himself and from whom he learned the rules of conduct the West demanded. Ford's use of landscape belies the "unhumanised vastness"; his plains and mesas reflect so emotional states that they become an extension of personality, totally inhabited, dominated by man and his values. Similarly, his attitude to the Indian reverses that of Fenimore Cooper and his contemporaries. Far from admiring and learning from Indians, the whites of Ford's films regard them as child-like savages, to be confined, protected and, if they rebel, disciplined. To Ford, the tame Indian is an uninteresting detail of life, and the wild Indian a figure of danger and mindless menace. Like all Ford's effects, his use of the Indian is precise and powerful, employed to convey shock and horror. This is apparent not only in the frequent evocations of Indian sadism typified by the scenes of murdered women and children (cf. *The Searchers, She Wore a Yellow Ribbon, Two Rode Together*) and of bound and tortured men (*Fort Apache*) which might be explained as mere documentary accuracy, but in scenes like the appearance of the Indian Blue Back in *Drums along the Mohawk*, a Frankenstein figure who materialises at the height of a thunderstorm; the chase by three Indians of the fleeing Henry Fonda in the same film, silhouettes again conveying the connotation of threatened death; the station-owner's wife in *Stagecoach* appearing outlined in the doorway to terrify the passengers; Chief Scar's shadow falling across the silent child in *The Searchers*; Stone Calf appearing howling, tomahawk upraised, in the firelight of *Two Rode Together* and the adopted boy foaming with rage in the same film; the drunken fury of Indian Joe in *My Darling Clementine*; these and many similar scenes suggest that Ford retains a fear and distrust of savages, rejecting the nineteenth century Rousseau-influenced admiration of

James Stewart faces Woody Strode during
TWO RODE TOGETHER

simple innocence that characterises American literary attitudes, preferring a prejudice based, one might suppose, on a devout Christian's terror of the alien and implacable Other to whom his beliefs have no value. Fenimore Cooper's vision is that of the explorer, Ford's of the missionary.

Ford shows little respect for Indian social customs or family life, as witness *passim* in *The Searchers* and *Two Rode Together*, and particularly his humorous use of the squaw Look in the former, where her devotion to Martin is used as an opportunity for broad farce. (Interestingly, the implication of that film that Indians have no regard for women, and that they are therefore fair game, also appears in *Stagecoach*; the station-owner's squaw Yakima was bought for a few horses, and when he hears she has ridden off it is the loss of his horse he laments, not of her.) Although Ford is cynical about the Indian capacity for self-control—drunkeness, condoned, even praised in an Irishman, is regarded in an Indian as vicious and reprehensible, cf. *Fort Apache, My Darling Clementine*—he grudgingly acknowledges their ability as warriors, since in this area as in no other their customs relate to white traditions of combat, or appear to do so. Conflicts between Indians and whites in Ford's films are almost always on the level of a pitched battle, preceded by elaborate warnings, parleys and tactical manoeuvres. The formalised encounters of *Fort Apache* are most aptly symbolic of this, and it can be no accident that Ford has all conversation carried on in Spanish, an acceptably aristocratic and "white" language. It is, one feels, the code Ford respects, not the people who live by it. Both extremes of this view are summed up concisely in *My Darling Clementine*. Indians appear only twice in this film, once at the beginning, where the drink-crazed Indian Joe (Charles Stevens) terrorises Tombstone until Earp subdues him with a rock ("What sort of town is this anyway?", he asks bitterly. "Selling liquor to Indians!") and the second time much later, when, emerging from the jail-house, Earp unconcernedly passes two old Indians squatting in the sun against the wall; a conversation in the foreground obscures them after a moment and they are not seen again. Ford, of course, intended no special significance in this, but the pattern of his attitude, and the familiar contrast between "good" and "bad" Indians is aptly conveyed.

6. The People Who Live : The Grapes of Wrath

In 1939, Darryl F. Zanuck, head of Twentieth-Century Fox, approached Ford to direct the film of John Steinbeck's Pulitzer Prize-winning novel *The Grapes of Wrath*, which pleaded the cause of the dispossessed farmers of Kansas and the mid-West. Turned off their rented land after decades of wasteful farming had reduced the area to a dust bowl, they migrated to the less highly-developed California, and became itinerant fruit-pickers and casual labourers, the hated, persecuted "Okies." Intrigued by the similarity between their plight and that of the Irish peasants who had been evicted by landowners in the famines of the late Nineteenth century, Ford accepted the assignment, even though a script had already been written by Nunnally Johnson, then amended somewhat by Zanuck, and a cast of Fox regulars assembled. Disturbed over the use of Fox contract player Jane Darwell for the central role of Ma Joad, matriarch of the wandering family, Ford and others associated with the film pressed for the role to go to Beulah Bondi, closer to Steinbeck's image of a gaunt, inflexible mother figure, a part she had played to perfection in Clarence Brown's *Of Human Hearts*. Zanuck refused to accept Bondi, though he did admit that his intention to cast as Tom Joad, the film's central character, either Don Ameche or Tyrone Power, Fox contract players, might be open to negotiation. Ford, appalled at both prospects, nominated Henry Fonda for the part, knowing that the actor was anxious to do it, a situation Zanuck shrewdly used to force the hitherto free-lance Fonda into signing an eight-picture contract with Fox. Although the company, with a string of inane comedies in the early Forties, failed to capitalise on its new star, Zanuck's manoeuvres to acquire him underline his skill as a politician.

Ford accepted the strictures of the project gracefully, and with an

John Ford on location for MOGAMBO

enthusiasm that grew as the film progressed. In Gregg Toland, he found a cinematographer who understood instinctively his undramatic photographic style, but who could observe it while making a personal contribution to the mood and ambiance of the film in a way Joe August never totally succeeded in doing. Toland's camerawork on *The Grapes of Wrath*, with its subtle linkages between exterior and interior scenes, its dramatic low-key close-ups and its counterpointing of Ford's unassertive but emotionally rich exteriors with perfectly judged effects of lighting and texture, withstands the most searching re-examination, repaying us with an increased admiration for this unique artist.

Johnson's script also deserves attention, not for its fidelity to the book, the bleak realism and almost Biblical anger of which it replaces with a melancholic compassion, but for the naturalistic edge he gives to the dialogue and characters. *The Grapes of Wrath* underlines even more firmly the fact that Ford is a director to whom the scriptwriter is vital, and one who relies on a writer to provide the dialogue and narrative structure which is then interpreted and expanded by the addition of detail in photography and performances. The published script shows that Ford departed from it very little in his shooting, varying it mainly by a flattening of dramatic peaks to provide the smooth flow of story he regards as ideal. Ford's personal signature appears not only in his interpretation of the dialogue, which is masterly, but in added gestures, effects of light, manipulations of natural events and a special use of landscape which cause us to see the words in a totally new way. One of the few outright additions to the original script is the final soliliquy of Ma Joad, where she reaffirms the durability of the workers. "We keep acomin'. We're the people that live. Can't nobody wipe us out . . ." Written by Zanuck, this was interpolated by him to sweeten the ending, replacing the brutal truth of Steinbeck's climax in which the deserted Rose of Sharon, half-mad with grief, suckles a starving boy from the breast that would have fed her dead baby, a grim incident out of keeping with the cautious optimism of Hollywood's political romances. Yet

Ford's sympathy with the inserted scene is undoubted; in one brief statement it sums up his whole faith in the infrangibility of community life and, more important to him, the insistent force of the family unit as an instrument of change.

In plot, *The Grapes of Wrath* is reasonably faithful to the original, most changes dictated by cinematic necessities and handled smoothly by Ford and Toland. Returning from four years in jail after killing a man, Tom Joad (Fonda) arrives at his Kansas home to find it deserted, vacated, as the half-mad fugitive Muley (John Qualen) explains, when the land company turned off its sharecroppers in order to farm the dying soil more efficiently. With the unfrocked preacher Casey (John Carradine), Tom finds his family at the home of his uncle John (Frank Darien), who has himself been evicted. The whole family: Ma (Jane Darwell), Pa (Russell Simpson), Granpa (Charley Grapewin), Granma (Zeffie Tilbury), Rose of Sharon (Dorris Bowdon), her husband Connie (Eddie Quillan), cousins Noah (Frank Sully) and Al (O. Z. Whitehead), the children Winfield (Darryl Hickman) and Ruthie (Shirley Mills), as well as Tom and Casey, set out for California on a wheezing truck loaded with their belongings. Although they make it to the San Fernando Valley, California is less than the promised land they expected. In a labour market overcrowded with other nomads, they are hounded, exploited by unscrupulous farmers and labour agents, persecuted by towns-people and the corrupt state police. The old people have died on the journey, and Connie leaves when the going gets tough, weaker elements dispersing as the family's strength is tested. Casey becomes involved in attempts by dissident workers to strike for better conditions, and is murdered by strike-breakers; Tom kills the man who clubbed Casey, but is himself wounded and made a fugitive. The family has a brief moment of peace at a government transient camp run on humanitarian lines, but the police discover Tom and he has to flee, telling his mother he will carry on Casey's work of fighting the exploiters. When he is gone, the family sets out again, the indestructible Americans.

The appropriateness of this subject to Ford is immediately apparent; the essential theme, of man's sacred relationship to his home and the soil, and his rightful anger at seeing these menaced, the emotional crisis of a family structure eroded and attacked by callous dispossession, its final triumphant affirmation of collective power, the Biblical resonances—the matriarchal figure of Ma Joad, to whom Ford attributes an aura of sacred power, making her the aging Virgin Mary, the woman who took Christ from the cross, and the echoes of themes like the prodigal son, the figure of the holy prophet (Casey) and of family strength. Ford's Catholicism gives to all these factors a cumulative weight of emotion that he was not to achieve again for many years.

Except for the sentimental and ubiquitous "Red River Valley" over the credits, the opening scenes of *The Grapes of Wrath* are among the most evocative and subdued in American cinema, with a cross-roads seen in the slanting sun of afternoon and lanky Tom Joad, hands in pockets, walking with tireless application out of the flat Midwestern landscape against a counterpoint of leaning telephone poles. Overhearing a conversation between truck-driver and waitress at a roadside pull-up, he asks for a lift, begrudged by the driver as contrary to the "No Riders" sticker placed on his truck by its owner, until Tom with logical directness says "A good guy don't pay no attention to what some heel makes him stick on his truck," a blunt statement of his instinctive belief that moral issues transcend conventional rules. Tom responds with similar truculence to the driver's searching questions about his past, revealing with grim humour the fact that he is just out of jail for murder, and smiling at the way the driver roars off at the tone in which he says "Homicide."

It is difficult to see Tom Joad in terms other than those in which Fonda and Ford draw him, so perfectly realised is the portrait of the man who must be both person and symbol. The set of Fonda's jaw, his relaxed but never servile slouch (what Whitman calls "the air . . . of persons who never know how it felt to stand in the presence of superiors"), his calm, direct eyes convey something that is private

Henry Fonda in the opening shot from THE GRAPES OF WRATH

and unique in Ford's work, the sense of moral worth, of instinctive honour, and of strength. Joad as Fonda portrays him lacks all those qualities another and more conventional actor and director would have brought to the role; honesty, intelligence, virtue, feeling. Tom, one senses, is not one for poetry, sunsets or abstract concepts. He likes a drink, is perfectly capable of killing a man who attacks him, and even quietly relishing the fact later. ("I laid him out with a shovel. Knocked his head plumb to squash.") Politics baffle him ("What is these 'Reds' anyhow? Seems everywhere I go someone's shouting about 'Reds'.") as they baffle all the farmers, especially Muley who, when his house is crushed by the bulldozer, can only think of shooting the president of the bank or "somebody who knows what a shotgun's for." Tom is no Lincolnian figure; significantly *The Grapes of Wrath*, a film about society in turmoil and disorganisation, lacks the perfect symbol of abstract authority common in other Ford works, although the Utopian government-run camp is a nod in this direction. Like Ethan in *The Searchers*, Ringo in *Stagecoach*, Ole in *The Long Voyage Home*, he is a transitional figure, both prophet and sacrifice, doomed to live shuffling between two necessities, his need for security balanced by the call of history streaming past his door. He has, fatally for his peace of mind, an instinctive identification with the tide he tries constantly to avoid, the rush of events seeking the place of rest which he, borne on its surface, can never reach, an identification perfectly summed up in his last farewell to his mother. "Maybe it's like Casey says. A fella ain't got a soul of his own, but only a piece of a big soul, the one big soul that belongs to everybody. And then it don't matter. Then I'll be all around in the dark. I'll be everywhere . . . Wherever there's a fight so hungry people can eat, I'll be there. Wherever there's a cop beating up a guy, I'll be there. I'll be in the way guys yell when they're mad— and I'll be in the way kids laugh when they're hungry and they know supper's ready . . . And when our people eat the stuff they raise, and live in the houses they build, why, I'll be there too."

Although Tom is the most powerful of these lost, transitional figures in *The Grapes of Wrath*, he is rivalled by John Carradine's Casey, the mystical ex-preacher who becomes an Okie Joe Hill, symbol of the fight for socialism and humanism, dominating every scene in which he appears, the role tailored perfectly by Ford to Carradine's lanky frame and folksy manner. Additional material has been added to the script to fatten Carradine's part, notably in the first scene between Tom and Casey, the latter reminiscing about his career as a preacher, including a sermon he once gave on the roof of a barn, straddling the roof-tree. Warming up, he recalls Tom's father arriving drunk at a service and so "getting the spirit" that he leaped into a bush and broke his leg. Though Casey merely mentions this in Johnson's dialogue, Carradine imitates it in the film by jumping over a fence, emerging dazed and embarrassed from the brush. Ford again uses gesture and movement to reveal a character trait, an almost insane ebullience in Casey that balances the seriousness of his ideals. One is reminded of Hank Worden's strange war dance in *The Searchers* that becomes a ritual dedication to the search.

Casey obviously touched a responsive chord in Ford, so affectionate is his treatment of the character. His casual attachment to the migrating family, he not wishing to impose himself, they responding to this sensitivity, after a worried look around the packed and teetering truck, with an instant invitation to jump aboard, has the quiet good manners Ford can so skilfully convey. Casey becomes thereafter a person of increasing charm, a benign spirit who sustains, protects but at last leaves the Joads to perform a similar service for the whole of society. His burial of Granpa by the roadside is particularly moving, and the simple valedictory he speaks is, as so often in Ford's films, less requiem than statement of principles. "If I was to pray I'd pray for the folks that's alive and don't know which way to turn," he says. "Old Granpa here, he ain't got no more trouble like that. He's got his job all cut out for him—so cover him up and let him get to it." This spirit of realistic humanism is echoed in his last speech in the tent by the bridge, before the strike-breakers club him to death, a statement underlining again that he is less an individual than a representation of social and moral force. "They think I'm the leader on account of I talk so much," he says, but the implication is that he at most reflects and re-states an unavoidable truth, while his death, and its immediate vengeance by Tom, suggests that he can never be killed, that in avenging him Tom automatically accepts responsibility for the task Casey set out to accomplish.

The third wanderer, Muley, is less important a figure, but one drawn with strong lines by Toland, who found the character's dramatic importance and John Qualen's defiant, child-like face a perfect opportunity for bravura camera-work. First seen in the abandoned Joad house, crouching away from the light of Tom's

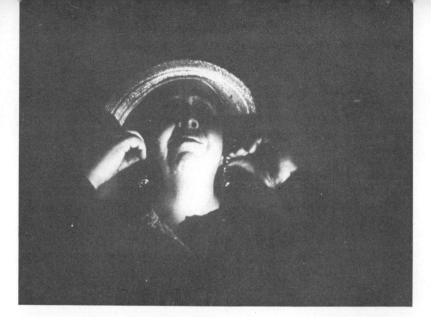

THE GRAPES OF WRATH Above : Jane Darwell before the mirror. Left top : Henry Fonda (seated) with John Carradine (at right) "They think I'm the leader". Left, bottom : John Qualen

guttering candle while the wind wails outside, he represents the fearful elements in the Okies, the ignorance and lack of flexibility that will destroy the weakest. His land gone and family split up, he has no life left; "I'm just an old graveyard ghost," he says, the bull-dozers having left him no place to go, no mental resources on which to fall back. Squatting in a pose often used in the film, especially by Casey, one which implies the animal nature of the Okies, the brutishness that can destroy them if their social fabric is allowed to crumble, he rages at the forces that have disinherited him, tearing at the earth as Granpa Joad does when he leaves his farm and when he dies, affirming his ownership. "It's ourn. That's what makes it ourn. Living on it and being born on it and dying on it." His shadow sprawls before him, the distorted image of a crouching beast robbed of that which made it a man, lacking the ambition that draws Tom and Casey up and on, searching for an answer.

Beside these powerful, almost Shakespearean characters, complex mixtures of man and symbol that bristle with enigmatic gestures, ambiguous actions and philosophical contradictions, Ma Joad, given considerable importance by the story, fails to convince. So bound up is her life with her family that she ceases to exist as a personality, coming fitfully to life only in relation to her son, for whose mystical ideas she is a convenient if uncomprehending sounding-board. One misses the sense of unbreakable will, so prominent in the book, which Beulah Bondi might have at least attempted to convey. Jane Darwell's undoubted talent is, however, displayed in one scene, an odd vignette which, perhaps because it refers not to her son but to her own obscured past life, and relies entirely on mood and mime, does convey a sense of loss at the destruction of the family and the support it provides. Before leaving their home, Ma goes through a box of mementoes, reading old letters and postcards before dropping them into the fire. She finds a tiny china dog, which she pockets, and a few trinkets, including a pair of cheap earrings. Calmly she puts them to her ears and looks up, remembering a scrap of happiness from her lost young life, a figure of indomitable calm, cushioned by her convictions. Then, sadly, she puts them into her pocket too, her past with them, and calmly covers the stove.

It is the character of Ma who, both physically and dramatically, dilutes the strongest feature of *The Grapes of Wrath*, the collaboration between Toland and Ford to create a visual sense of a dying America, reduced to the bare bones. When the film confines itself to the male players, the conjunction is complete and dramatically unassailable, an echo of "American Gothic" in the posing of figures in the landscape, the movement of men, objects and light across the

Russell Simpson and John Carradine in THE GRAPES OF WRATH

land. None of the actors used make-up and much of the film was shot in morning or afternoon, Ford following his long-standing inclination for slanting light. The influence this exercises over everything in the film's exteriors gives it an extraordinary truthfulness most noticeable in the first scenes, those with Tom at the café where he picks up a lift and in the sequence by the river, where Pa and John Joad wade reluctantly into the water, still in long underwear, an evocative image with echoes of a Biblical cleansing, of a triumphant immersion in the new life which the young accept joyfully, in contrast to the caution of the older generation. In the script, this incident was given

97

greater weight when the idiot boy Noah slips away from the party to return to the river and happily paddle in it while the others move across the desert, but the scene disappeared along with Ford's excision of Noah's feeble-mindedness, an aspect of personality he clearly finds disagreeable.

Toland comfortably adapted his style to Ford's, working closely with the director to create a work of remarkable cohesiveness. The shots that most stick in one's mind are naturalistic exteriors, but, as always, Ford is most at ease in dialogue scenes where the visuals are an emphasis to character rather than an end in themselves. Many of these are shot on the set, with little attempt to disguise the hollowness of the voices or the artificial light, unimportant to Ford by

'Cleansing' at the river in THE GRAPES OF WRATH

comparison with the necessity to create a carefully calculated effect. The long tracking shot on the conversation between Tom and Casey in the first reel is patently a studio scene, but Ford's care to suggest the flat yellow light of an approaching storm, his use of wind to stir the leaves and the dust, implying the emotional disturbance to come, an effect that reaches its climax in the gale that precedes and accompanies his return to the deserted house and his meeting with Muley, justify its artificiality. In the same way, his use of silhouette to show Casey and Tom, homeless and alone, wandering the land in search of a destroyed society, is a precisely judged theatrical effect that transcends conventional realism to touch the heart of his story. *The Grapes of Wrath* is neither Steinbeck nor documentary realism, but it *is* Ford.

7. Happy Families: My Darling Clementine, How Green Was My Valley

The word "family," like "tradition," "realism" and "American," is used by critics of Ford's films with an imprecision of which the director is seldom guilty. "Family" to us suggests the warmth of a basic relationship, the comfort of hearth and home, an unspoken bond of friendship and understanding. The family is static, settled, a building block of society whose worth depends on integrity and resistance to change. This view dominates American cinema, which in films like *A Tree Grows in Brooklyn, Mrs. Miniver, I Remember Mama* and *The Yearling* was at pains to emphasise the coherence a respect for family gave to society. Yet Ford shares none of this. To him, "family" is a concept more than a group of people, a dynamic, not a static institution, an instrument for change rather than for stability. His films abound with family groups, but those featured with any detail, like the Joads, are singled out for their force and power, just as his heroes are praised not for their virtue and integrity alone, but for their ability, whether by action or example, to assist society in a time of need.

Though there are few villains in Ford's films, and those who do appear are generally characterised by their self-interest and detachment from community aims rather than by overt evil, his work has many examples of families that work ruthlessly to disturb and destroy the smooth working of society, and an equal number of forceful families that intervene to foil them. The theme is foreshadowed in *North of Hudson Bay*, where Tom Mix's search for his brother, instigated at his mother's request, is complicated by Frank Campeau and his niece, with whom Mix has fallen in love. Henrietta Crossman in *Pilgrimage* is a mother who destroys her son's happiness until a meeting with another young man who has suffered through his mother's ignorance shows her the error of her ways. In *My Darling Clementine*, the Earp brothers are opposed by the Clantons, in *Wagon Master* the train is menaced by the Clegg clan, in *Two Rode Together* another Clegg family is active in destroying Guthrie McCabe's attempt to rescue the captives. Ford's families are most often seen in the act of organising or opposing some contrary force, and while *Four Men and a Prayer*, with its story of sons unearthing the organisation that destroyed their father, and *The Grapes of Wrath* with the Joads aggressively imposing themselves on an unwilling and unfriendly society show this attitude at its most obvious, it is explored more perceptively, and Ford's feelings about family more accurately conveyed in two of his most notable films of the Forties, *How Green Was My Valley* (1941) and *My Darling Clementine* (1946).

My Darling Clementine is one of Ford's most complex and moving films, open to a variety of interpretations. The story has a deceptive simplicity. The four Earp brothers—Wyatt (Henry Fonda), Virgil (Tim Holt), Morgan (Ward Bond) and James (Don Garner)—are riding through Arizona with a herd of cattle which is stolen by the Clanton family, led by Old Man Clanton (Walter Brennan), a crime during which the youngest brother is killed. The three Earps remain in Tombstone, Wyatt becoming marshal and the brothers his deputies. Doc Holliday (Victor Mature), who runs the town, likes the new marshal, and the men achieve a *modus vivendi* that is not greatly disturbed by the arrival of Holliday's *fiancée* Clementine Carter (Cathy Downs) with whom Wyatt falls in love. After a brief falling-out when Wyatt suspects Holliday of having been involved in the murder of James, the two families, with Holliday joining the Earps, fight it out at the O.K. Corral. All the Clantons are killed, as is Holliday, and Earp says goodbye to Clementine, promising to return after he has taken the news home to his father.

Despite this relatively simple narrative, *My Darling Clementine* bristles with intriguing features, many of them novel to Ford's work. Sexually, it is his most complex film. A homosexual attachment is implied, no doubt subconsciously, between Holliday and Wyatt, encapsulated in the latter's admiring response to his first glimpse of Doc, "A fine-looking man," but supported by Wyatt's solicitude for Holliday in his illness, his resentment of the other's mistress Chihuahua (Linda Darnell) and his nervous decision to take over Holliday's discarded *fiancée* who is, in a sense, the feminine aspect of Holliday's personality. The mechanics of courtship are conveyed with all Ford's skill, the elegant Wyatt, perfumed and impeccably dressed, walking cautiously into the hotel where Clementine is preparing to leave and nervously implying his desire for her, an approach that has its consummation in the famous scene where the couple, at a ceremony to consecrate the floor of a new church, dance, first gravely, then with increasing ebullience as the townspeople look approvingly on.

The true hero of the film, at least in the sense that Ford usually employs a hero, as martyr and good example, is Doc Holliday. It is he who sacrifices his life and happiness to maintain law and order, he who makes the vital decisions that eventually allow Wyatt and Morgan to clean up Tombstone and avenge their murdered brothers, he whose attitudes are more indicative of Ford's views about the dignity and responsibility of man than Wyatt's relatively direct ambitions. As such, Holliday relates closely to those figures in other

*Above : Cathy Downs, Victor Mature and Henry Fonda in
MY DARLING CLEMENTINE. Right : Cathy Downs and
Henry Fonda dancing*

Ford films—Casey in *The Grapes of Wrath*, Brickley in *They Were
Expendable*, Tom Doniphon in *The Man Who Shot Liberty Valance*,
the parson Gruffydd in *How Green Was My Valley*—who, with their
determination to respect their principles are intended as examples to
the audience rather than dramatic characters. Wyatt is the glamorous
central figure, but it is Holliday, the moral hero, whom the film's
characters admire and understand. A scene like that in which
Holliday, pitying the drunken actor Granville Thorndyke (Alan

Mowbray) who falters halfway through the "To be or not to be" soliliquy, completes the speech, emphasising movingly the significant phrase "to die, to sleep no more," gives to Holliday a dimension of feeling the merely agreeable Wyatt cannot command.

Despite the character conflict, the issues of *My Darling Clementine* are mainly familiae, with occasional nods towards minor themes like Ford's perennial interest in the influence of civilization on frontier values, suggested in the script by wondering comments like "Shakespeare, in *Tombstone*!" "Church-bells, in *Tombstone*!" The involvement of the Earp-Clanton feud in the civilising process is telegraphed in the opening scene where, out on the plains of Monument Valley, Ford's chosen site for vital moral disputes, the Earps meet nervous, calculating Old Man Clanton and his rapacious sons, the confrontation isolating under a cold winter sky the issues that will eventually kill most of them. "Rough country" Wyatt remarks phlegmatically of the windswept wilderness, its towering buttes assigning to the scene Ford's *imprimatur* of significance, and implying that, although this is a family fight, larger considerations are involved. Later, in a short scene beside the grave of the dead brother James (Ford meticulously re-creating a valley location with back projection and a complex foreground of shale slabs which also make up the burial mound), Wyatt comments, in a typical statement of principles, "We'll stick around . . . maybe we can help to make a country where kids like you can grow up safe." Clearly family honour is vital, but the conjunction of personal issues with the larger ones of civilization and law and order shows how little Ford cares about family unity and honour merely for its own sake, how concerned he is to show the family as a positive force, a social weapon to be used in ordering the world. The issues are crystallised by assigning to the Earps a pattern of neat, careful movement, disturbing nothing, providing a steadying force on those around them, and to the Clantons all the aspects of chaos; self-interest, wilful destructiveness, contempt for property.

The Earps argue against violence in even the simplest situations.

Regular and slowly-eaten meals, neat clothing, quiet conversation and easy movements make them the embodiment of conscious control and the law they represent. Wyatt protests even the breaking of bottles or glasses, takes great care to have his hair cut and oiled properly, leading to Ford's continuing joke of people imagining they can smell the desert flowers when it is in fact his hair-oil. He views with caution even so simple an interruption to routine as a social dance, and is magisterial, though quiet, in quelling a riot at the theatre when the promised artist does not appear and the crowd rebels in expectation of the usual replacement, the dreaded "bird imitators." Gestures like his trick of dropping his poker chips into his hat, then flipping it onto this head, and the odd game of balancing himself in his chair and supporting himself with alternate feet on the verandah post are not meaningless, but add to his character a visible order and economy of movement that has cumulative force. But although the Earps are diametrically opposed to the Clantons' way of life, similarities between their families and others in Ford's films are undeniable. In all cases, the father is evoked as the dominating head, controlling his sons in a way one seldom finds in real life. Old Man Clanton beats his boys into submission with a whip, treating them like undisciplined animals, and though the Earp father is not seen, his influence is overwhelming. The idea of "telling Pa" crops up often in the Earps' motivations; "How will we tell Pa?" is one of their first reactions to the death of James, shot by the Clantons in their robbery; Wyatt, on killing the Clanton boys, offers to spare the Old Man so that he can live with the knowledge of his loss "like our Pa will have to," and the final shot shows him and Morgan leaving town to "tell Pa," Wyatt turning his back, admittedly only for a short time, on his love for Clementine in order to carry out his duty to the abstract symbol of order.

"Pa" Earp and his importance point out the almost magical significance Ford gives to fathers. He does not see the family as a unit, but rather as an extension of a single personality. In *The Grapes of Wrath* this is stated explicitly when Pa Joad, a minor

The hill from HOW GREEN WAS MY VALLEY

figure, acknowledges that Ma "*is* the family," and mainly responsible for keeping it together. In *The Last Hurrah*, the sons of Skeffington and Cass are cretinous clowns by comparison with their powerful fathers. Old Man Clanton and Pa Joad occupy equally important roles in their families, as does Morgan in *How Green Was My Valley*, and in all his films Ford characterises sons and daughters as weaker, depending on the father, offering only additional force, never extra moral weight. This attitude is typical of Ford's doubt about the younger generation, to whom he is seldom prepared to concede any personality except in relation to some older figure. His young people depend always on a mature person of whom they are really an extension; *The Last Hurrah, Gideon of Scotland Yard, The Searchers, Wee Willie Winkie, Steamboat round the Bend* and *Pilgrimage* all hinge on such relationships, and a similar combination, combined with Ford's view of the family as a unit of change, dominates *How Green Was My Valley*, giving it a quiet force few of his films achieve.

Ostensibly *How Green Was My Valley* is about the destruction of a society, and of a family that is representative of that society, but in fact the real theme is a good deal less banal. As in *The Grapes of Wrath*, the family is not so much destroyed as encouraged to change, and in changing to dominate its environment, a process that detaches some members but ends with the purpose fulfilled. Richard Llewellyn's novel of life in an idyllic Welsh mining village at the turn of the century destroyed by the greed of the mine-owners and the pressure of industrial revolution was altered by Ford into an affirmation of the ability of men to exercise control over the world. At the beginning of the film, the Morgan sons have all emigrated, the father (Donald Crisp) is dead in a mine explosion and the youngest boy, who is also the narrator, is preparing to leave a valley that has been destroyed by indiscriminate mining. A flashback shows how this has come about. Poignant, one might think—but the effect is entirely the opposite. Ford, significantly, ignored the script's suggestion that the hands seen tying a bundle in the opening shot should be those of "a man about sixty," and instead made them young and skilful, giving to the decision of Huw to leave the valley a sense of beginning and not of ending. Throughout the story, we see the Morgans fighting to improve their lot, to crush the forces that would destroy them, to take over their world, and eventually they succeed, at the cost of some lives, and of the beauty they had once enjoyed. But since that beauty is never emphasised, it is of little dramatic importance. Most shots are interiors that concentrate on social and personal conflicts, and the few that do show the valley focus, like Ford's Monument Valley films, on the moral significance of its features rather than their beauty, so that the hills are used to represent difficult tasks mastered or, in the case of Angaharad's marriage to one of the mine-owners, a rise in status and a fatal detachment from community.

Through shrewd characterisation and direction, every outside force is shown as inferior to the Morgan family. The mine-owners, dominant figures in the book, are referred to in the film only in passing, and then shown as impotent, even comic. When Evans the owner calls on Morgan to ask for his daughter (Maureen O'Hara) as a wife for his son, he is shown in his formal clothes to be totally out of

Bronwen (Anna Lee) meeting the Morgan family in HOW GREEN WAS MY VALLEY

Rhys Williams and Barry Fitzgerald lead the wedding celebrations in
HOW GREEN WAS MY VALLEY

place in the Morgan home, while Morgan's receipt of the suggestion in bare feet makes Evans's formality more ridiculous. There is no suggestion that Morgan feels himself inferior; with Evans sitting nervously in his chair and Morgan pacing up and down before him, the dramatic emphasis is quite clearly placed. Later Evans tries to discipline Morgan for his involvement in a strike by forcing him to work in the rain, but Morgan is indifferent, and eventually the punishment is discontinued. Royalty cannot overawe the Morgans; they are invited to sing for Queen Victoria, and accept with equanimity, and even community dislike, that most potent of Fordian threats, disturbs them only marginally, Mrs. Morgan attending a midnight union meeting in the snow to harangue the miners and force them to admit their error in blaming Morgan for the strike. Morgan Senior's mastery of his own family is constantly emphasised, both in details of the ritual on which their life is based, and in the scene where the sons, refusing to accept their father's ruling on the issue of industrial justice, are forced to leave home. There is no suggestion that Morgan might relent, and the boys file quietly upstairs to pack their gear and move out, leaving only Huw (Roddy McDowall), the child whose allegiance Morgan gravely acknowledges when attention is drawn to it by a pointed cough, and whose relationship to his father seems close to the Fordian ideal. Morgan dies at last, but he cannot really be killed. The script recalls him for the last shot, and the commentary says, "Men like my father cannot die . . . They remain a living truth in my mind."

How Green Was My Valley is rich in those Fordian descriptions of ritual that do much to build up the image of an enduring social institution. The craft of mining is never shown as the direct cause of the valley's destruction which it clearly is, but as a noble calling and the life-blood of the community. The collection of wages, the custom of dropping the coins into the spread apron of Mrs. Morgan as she sits by the gate, the careful doling-out of spending money to the sons after dinner are shown in intimate, even loving detail. The ritual of "The Box" in which the family savings are kept is given special attention, with figures formally grouped in the lamp-lit room, patterns of light sprawled over the low white ceiling in one of Ford's favourite effects. Respect for "The Pit" is rivalled only by respect for "Chapel." Huw reverently removes his hat when passing the church and sidles past it as if the building contains a holy mystery on which one's back may not be turned, and mining, shown only in favourable details like the outbreak of singing as the miners march down the hill, the communal family wash to remove coal dust, and other ritualistic acts, is so glamorous that Huw, the intelligent, even intellectual narrator, automatically opts for a life in the mines rather than a full education. Implicitly endorsing this decision, Ford gives considerable weight to the scene in which two friends of the Morgan family call at Huw's school to beat up the teacher who has unfairly whipped the boy. Under the guise of "teaching" the man, the two miners knock him insensible, and this scene, with the lessons Dai Bando (Rhys Williams) gives Huw in defending himself, makes an overwhelming point that the only education worth considering is that in the exercise of physical force.

Life in the valley is recalled by Ford with a warmth and vitality usually reserved for his Irish films. The wedding of Ivor and Bronwen is an excuse for some lavish detail of community life and ritual, none of it in Philip Dunne's original script but improvised by Ford. Some details are echoes or anticipations of other films, like Morgan's impatient slapping of Ivor's hand as he fidgets in church, a direct parallel with Old Man Clanton's whipping of his sons when they terrorise the actor. Others show Ford's genius in extemporising detail to expand his action sequences and reflect the attitudes and ideals of his characters. At the wedding, Morgan, drunk, plays a game, balancing on one foot on a chalk line and performing tricks while reciting a nonsense rhyme, one of the non-competitive games Ford enjoys and directly related to Wyatt Earp's little exercise in balance in *My Darling Clementine* which shows him, like Morgan, to be totally in control. Later, the minister (Walter Pidgeon) arrives at the wedding unexpectedly. A drunken, presumably suggestive song is replaced by a more chaste tune and the minister, smiling, downs a glass of beer, automatically admitting himself as a member of the intemperate community by which he is surrounded. Having mastered mine-owners, their peers and royalty, the Morgans then seem to have taken on God, and beaten him too.

8. *They Cannot Change the Sea: The Long Voyage Home*

Immediately after the completion of *The Grapes of Wrath* in 1939 Ford began work on *The Long Voyage Home*, his first production for his own Argosy Films and the most important examination he had made of the pressures on men crowded together under combat conditions. The theme was to occupy him increasingly during the Forties, and to reach its peak of development in *They Were Expendable*. Encouraged by the fact that most of the characters in the four short plays by Eugene O'Neill from which the script was taken were European, Ford cast in the film some of the actors from the Abbey Theatre he had imported for *The Plough and the Stars*; Barry Fitzgerald and his brother Arthur Shields, Wilfred Lawson and Mildred Natwick, adding to them John Wayne, Thomas Mitchell, John Qualen and Ian Hunter. As a crew they represent a curious collection of opposites, both in accents and acting styles, but as Gregg Toland's remarkable photography dominates every other aspect of the production, disparities are not as obvious as they might have been.

O'Neill's plays, of which little remains in Dudley Nichols's script, were fragments of life at sea, seen, as usual for the playwright, as symbolic conflicts between man and his subconscious. "With their hates and desires men can change the face of the earth," an ambiguous title remarks, "but they cannot change the sea," accentuating Ford's belief that natural backgrounds should reflect the essential tone of the story. The script makes more specific the generalised nature of O'Neill's vision, localising the period at the beginning of the War, the ship as an English freighter, the "Glencairn," plying between South America and Europe with a cargo of munitions, and the crew as a collection of old salts with a wealth of wit and experience which they express at the slightest encouragement. Hoping to build up this humanist element, Ford works hard to remind us of the traditional seaman's life, the stern discipline that gives the sailors the only community they know and draws them back to sign up again after every voyage, but the conflict of this view with O'Neill's more psychological approach is never resolved. In its gloomy view of men isolated from the warmth of true community, *The Long Voyage Home* relates to Ford's "island" films and describes, as they do, the desperate pugnacity and humour which hides the desperation its isolated individuals feel. Its performances are also of high quality, and Gregg Toland's camera-work a unique excursion into visual imagery and the alternation of textures. Heavily-filtered high-contrast stock, hard side lighting and a relentless observance of the correct angle in the face of dramatic and narrative necessities make the film an essay in pictorial counterpoint, relating more to Constructivism or Cubism than to the director's humanitarian tendencies. To see *The Long Voyage Home* in a good copy, with the bronze texture and deep blacks of a nitrate print, is to realise again that Toland was one of the supreme visual stylists of the cinema.

Nevertheless, there are some jolting variations between style and theme in many sequences, including the opening, a Fordian use of "Blow the Man Down" over the titles succeeded by Toland's bravura handling of the first shots; a ship blocked black against the pale night sky in a typical foreshadowing of coming death, a sea as still and dark as oil, native women, coppered images, lolling sensuously against palm trees, one caressing herself in an agony of frustration as the ship with its cargo of men lies unattainable in the bay and the native chants drift out to taunt the frustrated sailors who come one by one to the rail and stare at the island. The tropical heat is as heavy as a damp cloth, crushing the men that lie sprawled on the hatch covers, their awkward poses expressive of boredom and erotic despair.

Inside, the ship is a racketting rust-bucket, bunks of jointed piping piled against the walls, bubbles of rust under the glossy black paint. Spotted in the light of the captain's torch as he searches for the tearaway Driscoll (Thomas Mitchell) who has slipped ashore against orders, the sailors are startled animals in a zoo, snarling, big-eyed, dazed by the light. Toland perfectly conveys the hardness of the ship, that it is iron and the men, despite their cynicism, only flesh. Hard shapes dominate every shot, even those of the sea and sky, water glinting like crushed glass, clouds clipped out of copper, the moon hard as a coin. Although Toland yields occasionally to Ford's admiration for flaring night shots similar to those Joe August conceived for *The Informer*, notably in the dock-side sequence where Smitty (Ian Hunter) jumps ship and is pursued by police through the bales and crates of the shipping yard, his style is uncompromisingly harsh and Cubist, a poetic evocation of industrial architecture. Ford, however, is too romantic an artist to discard entirely the broader levels of emotion. When the native girls, led by a Carmen-Miranda-like Rafaela Ottiano, board the ship with baskets of fruit and bottles of rum, the scene dissolves into a characteristic Fordian romp, sailors snatching up the girls and carrying them, squealing their protests, below, a fight breaking out, one girl watching with delight, a sudden wind whipping her blouse in that most personal of Ford's symbols for sexual desire or deep feeling, leading to the final almost balletic shot on the hatch cover as Jack Pennick smashes a bottle and quietly slashes the shoulder of a fighter. An ingenious alternation between high and low angles, careful staging of the incident among hard shapes of stairs and machinery enable Ford and Toland to achieve one of the film's most successful syntheses of action and image.

Despite this, there is an unfortunate soft centre to Ford's handling of the film's main sub-plot, revolving around Smitty, the incongruously well-spoken, clean and genteel British drunk who remains an enigma to the crew until, for reasons never adequately explained, they suspect him of being a Nazi saboteur, search his private papers looking for a bomb but find instead that he is an ex-Navy officer reduced by his weakness to serving as an ordinary seaman. The letter from Smitty's wife in which this information is contained suffers considerable re-writing from the O'Neill play, where it is brutally critical and ends with a rejection. Ford may not be completely responsible for Ian Hunter's stiffly formal playing, nor for his physical inappropriateness for the part, but the identification of Smitty with English honour and duty, culminating in his heroic death during an air raid on the "Glencairn" and a final hilarious shot with the Navy ensign superimposed over a lifeboat with Smitty's lifeless foot protruding from it as "Rule, Britannia" peals forth, is a clear example of Ford's inability to call a halt before his effect becomes overblown. Yet the episode of Smitty does have its examples of Ford at his best, most notably when, as the sailors realise how they have intruded on a private grief by reading his letters, and one man at the back sneaks away in a subtly appropriate touch, the bound and gagged figure of Smitty finds a curious peace, as if grateful that the secret is out, and that his sin of deception and refusal to share his life with the community has been forgiven. He strolls on to the empty deck. "All well, Smitty?" the man on watch calls, and Smitty, after a pause, says quietly, "All's well, Ole."

The film's second half, little related to the rest except in its characters, deals with the simple Swedish farm-boy Ole (John Wayne) and his attempts to leave the sea. A transitional figure like Tom Joad, Ole seems doomed to drift between opposing lives, committed to neither, sharing the sailors' idealised dream of settling down, but drawn like them to the only community he knows, the brutal cameraderie of shipboard life. When they dock, the other crew members combine to ensure that Ole carries out his intention to sail for Sweden, sewing his saved wages and steamboat ticket into his jacket, refusing him any liquor while constantly reminding each other, between drinks, that they must get Ole on his boat. As an exercise in tension this section bears comparison with *The Informer*, which in playing, appearance and photographic style it resembles. Ford peoples his phony London with Twenties grotesques; J. M. Kerrigan's sly and falsely amiable tout, Mildred Natwick, superbly raddled and maudlin as the prostitute who drugs Ole in an attempt to shanghai him, a blind violinist who plays "Shenandoah" for the sailors, and thugs and barmen who would not have been out of place in *The Threepenny Opera*. Plainly at home in this setting, Ford responds with the film's liveliest and most atmospheric scenes, culminating in Ole's rescue from the ship onto which he has been kidnapped, with a fight on deck among dozens of clanging metal drums.

Throughout this section, Toland's experimental genius with the manipulation of light is suppressed in favour of an Expressionist style recalling *The Informer* (and showing how instinctively Ford returns to that film's artificial approach), but in a short final sequence that, as epilogue and summation of the film's theme, is the most memorable of *The Long Voyage Home*, he is again allowed a free hand. Set in a secluded courtyard at the ship's side where a wind whirls discarded papers and pools of dust, it shows Donkeyman (Arthur Shields) watching the sailors, their money and high ambitions gone, straggle back to the ship to sign up once more. The only one to recognise the inevitability of the process and sign up himself in advance, Donkeyman compassionately understands the exhaustion in their step and the desperation in the dragging gait of Cocky (Barry Fitzgerald) as he returns flanked by two policemen. Toland alternates high and low shots, including some from under the gangway where patterns from the water skitter gaily on the planks, a malicious joke at the sailors' expense and a reminder of the eternal sea that reclaims them all, invoked once more in the film's final shot where, as Donkeyman hears Driscoll has been shanghaied aboard another ship while rescuing Ole, he tosses overboard a paper with the headline announcing that she has been sunk with all hands. The sodden paper catches briefly on the ship's hull, water from the slowly turning screws boiling over it, streaked with oil and bubbles, the dark headline announcing the death of a ship by violence, the only fate the "Glencairn" and its men can expect. This image resonates admirably with an earlier one, set in the same untidy courtyard, where Smitty's family visit the ship to collect his belongings. The black Rolls-Royce with its liveried chauffeur standing by the far wall, the slow pace of the veiled widow and the nervous curiosity of her white-faced

Returning to the ship from THE LONG VOYAGE HOME

children as they glance up at the sailors leaning over the side convey both the formality that follows death and the indifference with which these doomed men face the bitter realities of their calling. With their hates and desires men can change the face of the earth, but they cannot change the sea.

A battle scene from THEY WERE EXPENDABLE

9. One Man's War: They Were Expendable

To Ford, a war, even one in which he was personally involved, was assimilable into art only through its relationship to individual suffering, and in the integration of personal courage into a community effort. It is especially appropriate that his work during the Second World War should have been mainly supervisory, the production of some workmanlike documentaries for the Office of Strategic Services, which made him head of its newly-formed Field Photographic Branch, and the shooting, at personal risk, of the documentary *The Battle of Midway* (1942). Officially Ford's job was to photograph the work of guerillas, saboteurs and Resistance fighters in Europe for historical purposes and later assessment, though he seems mainly to have collaborated with his prewar colleagues, Gregg Toland, Dudley Nichols, Joe August among them, in the creation of some serviceable but unremarkable actuality films. Not unlike his own characters, Ford accepted readily the anonymity of service life and the necessity of bowing to its requirements.

His only personal film of the war was *The Battle of Midway*, which recorded the vital battle in which an Allied fleet turned back the Japanese task force threatening the southern Pacific and Australia. For this production, Lieutenant-Commander Ford USN was replaced dramatically by John Ford, film-maker. Before the battle started, Ford set up cameras in a dug-out on the island of Midway, and throughout the battle recorded the Japanese bombing, aerial battles and the damage done to naval installations and hospitals, as well as the gesture of some ratings in raising the flag during a bombing attack. This was later combined with footage shot by others of action on the aircraft carriers, and of the Air Force hunting down remnants of the Japanese fleet. Ford was wounded during the bombing and later lost the use of his left eye; to complete the documentary, other members of his team shot the funeral services of those killed in the battle, and other background footage. The result, quickly edited to eighteen minutes, became the first documentary of America's war effort. It was not until some weeks later that Ford was able to view the version of *The Battle of Midway* Twentieth Century-Fox and the Navy had prepared for general release, and when he did it was with dismay. To him, the poker-faced official commentary was unworthy of the men whose deaths he had recorded. Taking charge once again of the film, he wrote, with Dudley Nichols and James Kevin McGuinness, a new commentary, which he recorded with some of his "stock company." Sentimental and over-written, with Jane Darwell as an archetypal mother figure urging her boys into action, then lachrymosely demanding "soft white sheets" for the wounded, and Henry Fonda and Donald Crisp the stern voices of American grit and determination, the commentary, as more than one critic commented, clashed badly with the evident realism of the action footage, but as the first glimpse of the U.S. at war that American audiences had seen, *The Battle of Midway* was a commercial success, and received a patriotic Oscar in the 1942 Awards.

Clearly the war had a profound effect on Ford, and of all his accumulated honours that of Admiral in the U.S. Naval Reserve seems to be his most cherished. But, like Walt Whitman, he had been close enough to combat to feel the sting of personal loss, and to develop an uncritical admiration for the courage of many with whom he served. Ford's war was not that of battles and strategy, but of cautious forays in small boats, of units working alone, sustained only by their skill and a faith in eventual victory. Under the pressure of war, all the qualities Ford admired in American community life were revitalised and condensed, while the Navy, with its rituals and discipline, had an instant appeal to him. In his first production after the war, he crystallised his experience into a monumental and moving film.

His source was W. H. White's *They Were Expendable*, a brief documentary account of the exploits of Motor Torpedo Boat Squadron No. 3 and its commander, Lieutenant John D. Bulkeley, during the Philippines invasion and subsequent defeat of the American forces. It was this squadron that was chosen to ferry

General Douglas MacArthur out of Corregidor as the Japanese approached, and Bulkeley's feat of carrying the General, his family and staff in three PT boats through enemy-held waters to safety in Australia was one of the few victories in what was otherwise a depressing episode of American military history. Bulkeley was feted, and recalled to Washington to plan what was to become a strong U.S. Navy PT force. White's book, actually little more than an edited interview with Bulkeley's second in command, Lieutenant Robert Balling Kelly, the original of John Wayne's Rusty Ryan in the film, followed the fortunes of the squadron as it was destroyed by sabotage, dwindling supplies, official ignorance and futile actions against superior enemy forces until, of the original seventy-two members, only four, all officers, survived, the remainder having been taken prisoner or killed on Corregidor and Bataan. The tone of the book, and of Ford's film, is concisely summed up by Kelly in a resigned remark. "We little guys—the ones who are expended— never get to see the broad picture of the war, never find out the reasons back of the moves or failures to move. We only see our part— look up through the palm trees at the seamy side of it." This combination of bitterness and calm acceptance of duty is the keynote of *They Were Expendable*.

This film comes from the heart of Ford's work, not only in its typical characters and attitudes, but in its unashamed depth of feeling, its total response to the human tragedy of war. Its personal associations are a guarantee of this. John Bulkeley, on whom Robert Montgomery's character of Brickley is based, was a friend and shipmate in France, and Ford's salary was donated to a fund to build a recreation centre for veterans of his unit, many of whom— Montgomery, Joseph August, Jack Pennick—worked on the production. He claims today to have forgotten the film entirely, but one wonders how much this is an attempt to avoid discussion of what was for him a testing time. Before he returned to civilian life Ford, it seems, had something to get off his chest, and he expressed it with a characteristic honesty. One senses something of his attitude in a remark made by Petty Officer "Boots" Mulcahey (Ward Bond) in an early scene. Asked to make a speech on the retirement of a fellow non-com., he growls, "I'm not going to make a speech; I've just got something to say."

Ford says, in essence, that the war brought out much that was great in the soldiers and sailors who fought it, that whether they won or lost the important thing was that under the pressures of conflict men demonstrated the strength of society, the sustaining value of ritual and the durability of old virtues. On the surface, *They Were Expendable* is about a defeat, the worst America suffered in the war, but in fact the true subject is the defiant persistence of social institutions and the reassurance they provide in the face of total violence. As Lincoln is the ever-present symbol of this order in Ford's frontier films, so in *They Were Expendable* General Douglas MacArthur becomes the messianic figure of power and wisdom, all-knowing, holy. The sense of this extraordinary charisma to Ford appears in the opening title, an evocative quote. "Today the guns are silent. A great tragedy has ended. A great victory has been won. I speak for the thousands of silent lips, forever stilled among the jungles and in the deep waters of the Pacific which marked the way." Then immediately afterwards, over shots of torpedo boats curving on bright water, the explicitly Biblical tag "Manila Bay in the Year of Our Lord 1941" indissolubly links MacArthur with God.

That the film is not really about PT boats or the Pacific War is conveyed in the first sequence, with a general watching disinterestedly as Brickley and Ryan demonstrate the abilities of their frail craft in some impressive exercises. "They manoeuvred beautifully," an aide concedes, but his general brushes the boats off with a remark that he "prefers something more substantial." Yet the sequence's most significant shot is that in which the general ignores the stiffly drawn-up personnel of the unit awaiting inspection, instantly connoting his lack of interest in Brickley's boats with a contempt for Naval ritual and, like Colonel Thursday and his distaste for cavalry customs, sharply characterising himself as unsympathetic, and wrong in his estimate of the squadron's capabilities. The incident also foreshadows the primary theme of the film, the way in which Navy discipline sustains Brickley and his crews under almost intolerable pressures. Even when Ryan bitches about the frailness of the boats and the hollowness of his first "command," this is not felt, a brief suggestion of rivalry between the two leaders that may, like an important final scene, have been added at Wayne's request to give his part more "bite."

The raid on Pearl Harbor, like most of the battle action in the film, happens offstage, intruding only by degrees into the formal perfection of Navy life at Manila. In the Non-Commissioned Officers' Mess, Mulcahey and the other ratings are gathered around the piano, singing Ford's favourite Navy tune ("The Monkeys Have No Tails in Zamboanga") in celebration of the retirement of Doc Charlie (Jack Pennick). For the benefit of some younger members, Mulcahey endorses the virtues of Navy life ("It means service, tough and good") while elsewhere, in rightful superiority, Brickley, Ryan and two incognito admirals relax in formal whites at the Officers' Club. When the news of the Japanese raid comes over the radio, Mulcahey brusquely orders it cut off as it interrupts his speech, but the admirals, all-wise, receive the facts quietly at their table and instantly take command. Ryan tears up his resignation from the unit and, in a curiously touching detail, the Japanese singer, who hears the announcement while knitting in the shadows, sings an impromptu "God Bless America," a ritual dedication for departing warriors as the officers file out to take up their duties.

Throughout the following scenes, authority continues to be segregated, Ford implies quite fittingly, from those who fight, the majesty and holiness of command accentuated by scenes of restless junior officers awaiting their orders shot from their point of view, the strategists seen distantly in their command post, voices muffled or inaudible, while lieutenants, Brickley included, kick their heels in the corridor. When he at last persuades a friend to carry a message into the holy of holies (one imagines with what contempt Ford views the Hollywood convention of the young officer bursting in with a "Now look here, Admiral . . ."), he receives a direction to patrol the harbor and run errands. Unsatisfactory as he finds the order, Brickley obeys it without question, even criticising Ryan when he vents his frustration not in words but by booting a convenient bucket. "Does that help?" Brickley asks, and when Ryan, storming out, snaps "Yes!", Brickley, alone in the command post and therefore providing no bad example to his juniors, kicks it himself. The shrewdness with which Ford outlines, in actions and gestures like this, the strict stratification of naval command and the rules, personal and formal, that govern its working is a remarkable example of his skill in implying social structures through visual and spoken details. Ingeniously expressed where Brickley waits for his orders in the admiral's outer office, the importance of the "chain of command" as an abstract symbol of order and discipline is emphasised once again in a later scene, when the retreating commanders decide to evacuate the Philippines and move south to Corregidor. As the admiral (Charles Trowbridge) allocates tasks in his makeshift headquarters, a low-roofed Nipa hut with bamboo blinds restraining the bright sun, Brickley's men wait calmly below the verandah, conscious, as we are, of a rightful sacrifice of their individuality in favour of a concerted, if little understood group effort.

Shortly before, in a half-shadowed scene in the wrecked headquarters which recalls in its still patterns of light the splashes of latticed sun that crawl over the ceiling of the command hut, the admiral has expressed to Brickley, in one of the film's most important conversations, the philosophy by which all of them live. "You and I are professionals," he says. "If the manager says sacrifice, we lay down the bunt and let somebody else hit the home run. That's what we were trained for and that's what we'll do." With these guidelines, and with the need for, even the desirability of heroism negated by the admiral's carefully stressed endorsement of strategic withdrawal, Brickley's unit becomes just part of the debris of defeat. Occasional raids, one of which, on a destroyer, goes disastrously wrong, are the sole moments of action in what is otherwise a tedious round of maintenance and patrol, but the sense of a common purpose sustains the men and nourishes their group spirit. It is to be expected that Ryan, the unit's maverick and fire-eater, played with engaging energy by Wayne, should move outside this strict pattern, and, when he visits the hospital on Corregidor, meet and fall in love with a nurse, Sandy Davis (Donna Reed). Ryan, to Ford the "other" world of emotion and civilian individuality, becomes increasingly important as the film progresses, recalling another set of traditions, those of American home life, to preserve which the war is being fought.

Two sequences, among the most moving the director ever created, accentuate these apparently conflicting but actually mutually dependent senses of community. The first follows Ryan's treatment at the hospital. Convalescing from the minor operation and with his arm still in a sling, he visits a staff dance to apologise to Sandy for his earlier rudeness. Couples shuffle to a muffled phonograph that croons a minor and inextinguishably Forties melody while outside the palm trees droop motionless in the stifling night. Sitting on a hammock— "Just like home," Ryan comments, recalling warm Ohio evenings and porch swings—they watch the distant gunflashes, which Sandy wryly compares to fireflies, but notes with harsh realism, "Each night, they come closer." They discuss their homes, and prewar America. Ryan puts his arm around her, embracing the symbol of his lost world, and they sit silently together. Brickley climbs the steps out of the darkness, watches the couple for a moment and quietly turns away. "It can wait," he says when Ryan notices him and asks what is happening; the instinctive courtliness of all Ford's aristocrats showing through, but the brief moment of rest is over. Inside, the record changes to "Goodnight, Ladies," as Ryan and Brickley go back to war.

This evocation of the civilian community through its rituals is answered later by Sandy's visit to Ryan's base and her experience of Naval formalities. In the first striking shot, taken from the verandah looking down the steps, a jeep with a red cross on its bonnet moves

Mulcahey (Ward Bond) and confederates singing "Dear Old Girl"
from THEY WERE EXPENDABLE

into frame, then drives on, revealing Sandy standing slumped with fatigue on the other side of the dirt road, her shadow lying across and seeming to be crushed by the incised tracks of the vehicle, an effect recalled from *The Grapes of Wrath* where the bulldozer that demolishes Muley's home grinds over the shadows of his family. Sandy's exhaustion and sense of defeat is apparent in her movements, but as she is ushered up the steps and into the officers' primitive mess, the ritual of hospitality revives her. She is introduced formally to the officers as "Lieutenant Ryan's guest"; candles light the thatched hut as the cook serves a meagre supper and under the floorboards

Mulcahey and two confederates harmonise on "Dear Old Girl." The chatter of table talk, the presence of a woman, the conscious return for sustaining energy to the power of ritual revives them all, with Sandy installed among the candles, radiant as a saint. When Brickley withdraws after the meal and the steward understandingly blows out the candles, leaving Ryan and Sandy sitting alone in the dark, still at their places, one senses that, though a few feet separates them, they are linked by the atmosphere the occasion has produced. It is a tragedy that, in TV screenings of the film, these scenes are among those most often cut, depriving it of a subsidiary theme indispensible to its message.

If Ryan and Sandy suggest the cause for which the war is being fought, two further scenes, both set in the Corregidor underground hospital where Sandy is a nurse, dramatise the cost of battle in terms of human suffering, and the reality of death that makes doubly poignant the hard humour of the PT men. Without the hospital scenes, the wisecracks of Mulcahey and Doc Charlie would be merely trivial, but throughout this long film even the simplest joke has its significance in the overall effect. Although apparently unconnected, some scenes set up an ingenious mutual tension. Refused permission to go on a raid because of his infected hand, Ryan storms into the hospital, a convincing recreation of Corregidor's Malinta Tunnel, reluctantly stays overnight when the wound proves more serious than he expected, and is in the underground bunker when casualties begin coming in. Ford's depiction of the scene is sweepingly theatrical; lights flickering and dying as explosions shake the buried hospital; operations carried out by the light of a torch as a demonic wind, like the gale of *The Quiet Man*'s love scene, flaps the sheet held up to protect the wounded man; the horrific full-face shot of a man, blind behind bandages, smoking a cigarette with trembling hands. When it is over, the nurses, calmness hiding their fatigue, walk off down a dark tunnel, only cigarette smoke remaining behind in the damp air, an image whose emotional vibrations defy exact analysis. Ford follows this with the aftermath of the raid in which Ryan was unable to participate. As his crew stand sadly by, the victorious boat returns with a broom tied to its masthead, traditional signal for a victory, and the survivors crowd around to retail stories of the dangers they faced. With studied insolence, Ryan's crew pass them off as of little account. "Was this recently? Oh, this morning. That reminds me, Slug; your laundry's ready. What a pity you missed breakfast too." The talk is halted, but not chilled, by the bringing ashore of a rating who has been killed in the skirmish, the body draped in the ritual flag. The humour, Ford implies by placing it between two scenes of death, is

Donna Reed as a nurse in the Malinta Tunnel from
THEY WERE EXPENDABLE

The dying Andrews (Paul Langton) being visited in hospital from
THEY WERE EXPENDABLE

part of the system too, a vital palliative to the constant danger and recognised as such by the men.

This is stressed yet again in the second hospital sequence, where the officers visit the wounded Andrews (Paul Langton), having been told beforehand that he has only a few hours to live. Ford's touch is everywhere; in the shadowy tunnel, the dying man sequestered behind a screen with light spearing out into the darkness; in the careful management of sound levels so that their noisy good humour as they burst in on him, by comparison with the solemn inaudibility of the earlier shot where they are told he will soon die, gives to their

The shadowy tunnel of the hospital from
THEY WERE EXPENDABLE

jokes a false over-emphasis, the grin of a skull. Without this contrast, there would have been far less poignancy in the exchange between Andrews and Brickley when the others have left. "Nice act you boys put on," the dying officer says, both men instantly abandoning what they have recognised all along as a pose, and the commander quietly arranges the business that is his reason for going there; the letters to wife and family, the last requests, the final stiff goodbye. This, the most heartbreaking duty of command, discharged, Brickley rejoins his men, silent in the tunnel and silhouetted in a foreshadowing of their friend's death. Passing through the group, he leads them out into the night. The conventional war drama would make this scene an unimportant interlude, spacing between the battles and banter, but to Ford the inter-relation of public and private duty, the value of rituals entered into without deception on either side are what the film is about, just as the details of Navy iconography—the broom at the masthead, the sign "Officers' Club" hung on their palm-thatched hut, the painted list of actions lying charred but still erect on the dock—are potent evocations of their faith in the code of their chosen calling.

It is more than halfway through the film before the instigator of

General MacArthur (Robert Barret) arrives aboard the PT boat from THEY WERE EXPENDABLE

their actions and the reason for their existence makes his appearance and, as in all Ford films, the event is treated more as a visitation from some superior being than the passing of a mere general. To Ford, MacArthur is a figure of immense emotional and moral potency, not merely a tactician and commander but the embodiment of the system for which Brickley, Ryan and their men fight and die. So analogous is he to Christ, as the opening title suggests, that he is never referred to by name, but invoked obliquely as "Command Personnel." It is not until the scenes leading up to the midnight debarkation from Bataan that we realise Brickley has been singled out to transport MacArthur and his staff to Australia, and even then the event is handled with a reverent detachment that would be ludicrous if it did not have behind it Ford's unashamed admiration. In dim moonlight and extreme long shot, a woman and boy leave a boat and walk along the ricketty wharf, followed by the unmistakable figure of MacArthur in familiar peaked cap and overcoat. "The Battle Hymn of the Republic" swells as he boards the PT boat, a dramatic effect cleverly terminated when an awed rating snatches off his gob cap and stutters "Will you autograph my hat?" Mulcahey throws up his hands but the general of course obliges, a Fordian touch of humanity in the great rather than a mockery of the not excessively modest MacArthur.

With MacArthur gone, the retreat becomes a rout, though, despite the increasing dilapidation of its boats, losses from sickness and injury, and the concerted attacks of the Japanese, the squadron retains its cohesiveness, confidence and sense of humour. Equipment is scrounged with a ruthless use of the "old boy network," involving in one case the blackmail of a colleague who, unmoved by pleas from Brickley and Ryan for half his stock of torpedoes, is petrified by the former's apparently innocent question, "Snuffy, who was it played the lead in *Tess of the D'Urbervilles* at the Academy in 1932?" As he turns slowly around Ryan adds "And does your crew know about it?" Although the last sections of *They Were Expendable* are deeply emotional, the treatment is devoid of extremes. *Motifs* from earlier in the film recur, distorted or poisoned by defeat, and the ritual so central to the story often lacks integral elements. When a church is found for the burial of two men killed in an attack, Ryan finds that the priest is injured and in hospital, and is forced to complete the formalities himself. Ryan's speech, ingenuous and embittered, sums up the disorientation all of them feel at the loss of the Navy's ritual institutions. Glancing bleakly at the two bare coffins, Ryan comments that Navy men deserve to be buried with full military honours—a flag, a firing squad—"but in war you've got to forget these things." In lieu of a prayer, he recites a poem; one of the men liked poetry. It is Stevenson's "Requiem"—"Home is the sailor, home from sea/And the hunter home from the hill"—the bitter tone in which he delivers it and the earlier renunciation of Naval tradition making it especially disturbing, more so when taken in conjunction with the scene that follows, where the funeral party bursts into a deserted bar and sullenly sits in the gloom drinking beer. The radio is playing the tune to which Ryan and Sandy danced on Corregidor, but it is interrupted by an announcement of the surrender of Bataan. The speaker quotes MacArthur's remark "Men who fight for liberty are more than flesh but they are not steel," the truth of this evident in the weariness of those who listen and then return to war.

Only the power of their discipline and rituals remains to nourish resistance. As the Japanese close in, the squadron's last boat is commandeered by the Army. Before it disappears, incongruously perched on a truck, a rating snatches its flag, an instinctive affirmation that emboldens the men. In a scene central to the final section of the film (and, like many important details, often cut for TV) the owner of the boatyard where the PT boat was under repair (Russell Simpson) refuses to join the retreat. "I worked forty years for this," he says tersely, "and if I leave they'll have to carry me out." Settling himself down with a jug of whisky and his rifle on his knees, he awaits the invasion, and Ford on the sound track brings up "Red River Valley," Ma Joad's *leitmotif* and a symbol to him of the strength

The boatyard owner (Russell Simpson) settles down to wait for the Japanese in THEY WERE EXPENDABLE

of American conservatism. After defeat, the unit is broken up, Brickley and Ryan flown, against their will, back to America to build up a force of PT boats later to have a decisive effect on the war. Mulcahey, limping on a crutch but indestructible, is put in charge of the remnant of the company that Ryan attempts to rejoin just before he flies out, only to be recalled by Brickley with a terse reminder of his duty; "Who are you working for, yourself or the Navy?" As the plane takes off, roaring over the survivors limping along a moonlit beach towards capture or death, "The Battle Hymn of the Republic" rises, and superimposed on the image is the title

"We Shall Return," the unbreakable promise of a military Second Coming and the eventual re-establishment of community.

They Were Expendable is the most deceptively episodic of Ford's films and, despite the championship of critics like Lindsay Anderson at the time of its release, one often disregarded in assessments of the director's work. "Deceptively episodic," for in fact there are few films in which Ford's grasp of construction is so evident, and in which he employs so economically his understanding of the effects to be gained by relating apparently minor scenes to each other. Heroics are kept to a minimum, and the visual bravura of the two battles, directed by second-unit director James C. Havens and Robert Montgomery, is out of place in the story's even tone. One senses Ford would have been happier had there been no military action at all. Joe August's pale, sunny images lack the strong contrasts of earlier Ford/August collaborations, but the total impression is all the more moving for this restraint. Silent groupings of defeated men in their wrecked headquarters or around the bed of a dying comrade convey perfectly the sense of "the ones who are expended", while the landscape of sad, palm-fringed beaches, lonely creeks and jungle trails shows nature echoing the lassitude of defeat.

The essential mood of the film is not easily crystallised, and critics have increasingly been forced back on the over-simplification that it is a story of gallantry in defeat, but again Whitman came closest to isolating the atmosphere Ford evokes. In *Vigil Strange I Kept On the Field One Night*, Whitman describes how, after a battle in which his friend has been killed, he returned to the body and remained by it all night, grieving but calmed by an almost mystical peace. "Long there and then in vigil I stood, dimly around me the battle-field spreading/Vigil wondrous and vigil sweet there in the fragrant silent night/But not a tear fell, not even a long-drawn sigh . . ." In film and poem the subject is not defeat, nor even grief or a sense of revenge, but the resources that man can find in himself when faced with loss, and the value of a shared body of experience—for Whitman the ancient religious ritual of the vigil by the dead, for Ford the in-

Survivors limping along a moonlit beach in
THEY WERE EXPENDABLE

grained usages of military discipline—when everything that sustains
a man has gone.

Ford adhered closely to White's book and its accounts of actions
and evacuations, and though much drama has been pared down to
create the characteristic Fordian fabric, a surprising amount of
documentary detail from Kelly's report remains. The romance of
Ryan and Sandy is based closely on Kelly's association with a nurse
called Peggy, and scenes like that in the Malinta hospital, with gusts

of wind from the bomb concussions, and operations carried on in the light of a torch, are recorded by him with almost shooting-script accuracy. Descriptions of the conditions under which the squadron lived are followed to the letter, as are details of discipline and living conditions on Corregidor and Bataan.

Ford's inventions for the story are predictable, given his known attitudes; the funeral at which Ryan speaks, the *motif* of youth and age combining to carry on the tradition of service with young ratings deferring completely to the old, and the sentimental farewell to the enlisted men who must remain on Bataan all have their counterparts elsewhere in Ford's work. A major change, and the hardest to justify, if not to understand, involves the evacuation of MacArthur. This exploit, with its combination of daring and superb seamanship on the part of Bulkeley and his men, is barely mentioned, discarded in a brief shot of PT boats under speed at night and the embarkation and debarkation of MacArthur. In White's book it is the climax and point of the story, although like Ford he uncritically accepts many erroneous statements about the event. MacArthur, despite claims that he evacuated only key personnel with no regard for rank, actually packed the boats with cronies, including his child's Chinese nurse, a number of generals and his personal public relations man. The only man of the twenty one below the rank of Captain was a sergeant who was secretary to one of the generals. In addition, the trip was complicated by the sea-sickness of the passengers, many of whom cut poor figures to the Navy men. The falsification of Mac-Arthur's image to sustain the charisma with which, in Ford's mind, he was surrounded, is characteristic of his preference for myth over reality in all his historical films, but seems here less justifiable than his deification of Lincoln, since the subject is so much less deserving.

*Ford rehearsing the entrance into Bar-le-Duc for WHAT
PRICE GLORY?*

10. The Profession of Arms: What Price Glory

Few of Ford's films have suffered the critical extinction of his 1952 production for Twentieth Century-Fox of *What Price Glory?*, a re-make of Raoul Walsh's 1928 film that in turn had been adapted from a successful Twenties play. Starring James Cagney and Dan Dailey as the feuding First World War Marines Captain Flagg and Sergeant Quirt, it had the advantage of expert playing from both the principals and members of Ford's stock company like Jack Pennick and William Demarest, as well as some of the most attractive low-key colour photography the ingenious Joe MacDonald ever produced. Yet it remains an unlikable film, amusing, tightly directed but unsatisfactory for reasons that tell us a lot about Ford and his attitudes. *What Price Glory?* is a textbook of formal direction technique, with Ford totally in control of the story's awkward combination of pacifist polemic, romance and knockabout farce. The long-standing friction between Quirt and Flagg expressed in ritualised fist fights that alternate with equally formalised salutes and orders, the romance with French girl Charmaine (Corinne Calvet) who is the apparent point of disagreement, the war scenes with their odd balance of tight action and emotional soul-searching; all involve a degree of management and cinematic engineering that one would have imagined Ford, with his studied avoidance of plot, lacked. The film dramatises what a fine technician Ford is, but underlines that, in his work, involvement is everything.

The opening scenes show Ford on familiar ground. Soldiers with haggard faces straggle out of a battered landscape to the "Marines' Hymn" and "The Battle Hymn of the Republic," used again to suggest that military failure and even death do not destroy *esprit de corps*. Flagg leads his shambling troops into the little town of Bar-le-Duc but, as they see a polished group of French soldiers awaiting them, straightens them up, forms ranks and marches them proudly

into the square. The gesture is typical of Ford, both in the indication of ritual as a source of strength and visually in MacDonald's low afternoon light, but any warmth is chilled by the precision of cutting, the correct but lifeless alternation of trumpets, uniforms and the opposing ranks of soldiers. A similar flatness is apparent in a later bar scene, Calvet singing a song to the soldiers as she teases one of them (Jack Pennick) with some fraudulent vamping, gasps with admiration as a boy swallows a lighted match and produces it, still lit, on the end of his tongue a moment later, and generally beguiles Flagg's command. Detail follows detail with such speed, such close attention to the direction of individual actions, that the warmth Ford always infuses by careful pacing or by uniquely personal touches of emotion is lost, the technique too apparent to involve us.

Later gestures of humanity suffer equally from mechanical handling, so that the sentiment is *gauche* or totally unfelt. There is little emotion in Flagg reviewing the new replacements, snarling at one a question as to where he was born and receiving a whispered "Providence," half reply, half prayer, with the bellowed "Rhode Island" as a late desperate addition, in the death of popular Lewisohn (Robert Wagner) that extracts from Flagg a fit of sobbing which, shown only in his heaving back, does not convince, or even in the film's centre-piece where a dying soldier taunts Flagg with his heroics ("There's two minutes to go and we need a hero. What price glory now?"). The suggestion from a soldier that his commander does not have the complete right to order the death of his men is alien to Ford, reflecting doubt as it does on the holiness of military discipline, and even the soldier's later death, reeling out of the dugout in bandages to battle on, and Ford's imposition on the scene of a syrupy hymn cannot neutralise his distaste with the whole situation. The scenes that have most crackle are those between Quirt and Flagg, because in these Ford falls back on his delight in ritual. Quirt

Opposite : two scenes from WHAT PRICE GLORY? Above : Flagg (James Cagney), Charmaine (Corinne Calvert) and Quirt (Dan Dailey). Below : "Providence" Flagg inspects the troop.

bawling his replacements through close order drill, empressing critical bystanders into the squad, marching another critic off a bridge and into the river; these incidents play on the comforts of discipline and emphasise its complete acceptance by all right-thinking Marines. Even Flagg's fights with Quirt are to a formula laid down in some unofficial book of rules. When he first reports to his old adversary, Quirt marches in, grabs a piece of chalk and marks a cross on the floor. Flagg does the same, they square up, Quirt is knocked down, picks himself up, puts on his belt, salutes and formally announces both his arrival and desire for a transfer in the same breath. The ritual of chalk, belt and fight, the formality of their language as they engage in lavish compliments and insults during a drinking match for the hand of Charmaine, the studied respect for each other's professional ability that is undiminished by Flagg's warning to the men that Quirt is a drunk, a cheat and a rake; all these emphasise that discipline and ritual must be the basis of even the most fundamental relationship between individuals, and especially those in military service.

Throughout the film, cameraman MacDonald is a useful ally to Ford, enriching even the flattest actions with superb pictorial values. Clearly Ford depended on his collaborator, especially in shots like that in which, as Flagg stands, apparently alone, in his office, Charmaine reveals her presence in a reflection that grows in the mottled glass of the window, as Olivia Pennell's shadow rose silently on the gravestone in *She Wore a Yellow Ribbon*. The slanting light of morning or dusk is made more than a subtle background detail, but featured as a dramatic effect, showing up Quirt's breath as he drills his men or flashing on the liquor that spurts from a bottle as aide Henry Morgan pounds with its base on the sergeant's door. An elaborate use of crane and dolly, more reminiscent of Lewis Milestone than Ford, dominates the film's main battle scene, a long track over silent graves to a field of grass that abruptly emits a whistle, the figure of Flagg appearing a moment later from where he crouched, followed by his whole platoon. The most elaborate exercise in a combination of visuals and action occurs at the climax, where Flagg and Quirt compete for Charmaine in the darkened café, first with a drinking match, then a hand of poker. Alert to useful detail, Ford accepts the presumably accidental breakage of Flagg's glass when he clinks it to Quirt's bottle, and has Cagney, when setting up his next drink, reflectively spit out a piece of broken glass. As the lights go down during an air raid and the two men sit at the table over their cards, low-key light from a lamp gives Flagg an almost *Grand Guignol* look as he bluffs Quirt out of the girl, a scene that dissolves into pure melodrama as the sergeant overturns the lamp and runs into the night, Flagg laughing maniacally in the dark room, lit only by the flash of passing headlights, until the lamps come on again to reveal the implacable figures of his staff sternly surrounding him. Ignoring his pleas that he is "sick of wandering" and wants "to sit in one place and never get up," they draw him back to the war.

That a film with so many of the basic elements from which Ford builds up his atmosphere should be lacking in force and deep feeling is an index of his dependence on a moral precept embodied in the material and an emotional understanding and enthusiasm for the lesson on his part. The play *What Price Glory?* was severely pacifist, and even the imposition of rough comedy by both Walsh's script-writers and Ford's could not obliterate the essential conflict between the warmth of comradeship and the inhumanity of war. Ford, who does not see war in these terms, attempts with strongly featurist direction to divert attention from the point, to put the emphasis on action, comedy, romance, but the experiment could never succeed, since Ford refuses to despise a soldier's motives or find fault in the military life. It is only at the end, when Flagg, marching back to war, says with a certain pride "There's something about the profession of arms, some kind of religion you can't shake," that the ring of true Fordian sentiment is heard. Here, at least, was a statement with which he could wholeheartedly agree.

11. Pilgrims: The Searchers, Two Rode Together

Is there any more American film than *The Searchers*, any work that more concisely sums up the dichotomy in American consciousness between the pioneer and the businessman, the soldier and the farmer? In its extraordinary economy, its efficiency of technique, the memorable playing of its principals and supporting cast it is perhaps Ford's most perfect philosophical statement. Based on an Alan Le May story called *The Search*—the title's personalisation is typical of Ford—which had as its original setting the Rocky Mountains, Frank Nugent's script, written with Ford in mind, uses both the quintessential Monument Valley landscape and the skilful Ford stock company, led by John Wayne. As Ethan Edwards, the wandering Civil War veteran who spends five years searching for a niece kidnapped by Indians, only to find that he and his task have become irrelevant, anachronisms in a world that has changed as his search never did, Wayne creates a character who is the summation of the wanderers he played in other Ford films, a lost cavalier whom we both sympathise with and dislike, while his dogged journey across the American landscape, indifferent to both its beauty and danger, identifies him with the pilgrim aspect of Ford's essential hero.

The Searchers is doubly interesting as a source of study because of its similarities to *Two Rode Together*, Ford's 1961 Columbia production undertaken as a favour to Harry Cohn and, although lacking any great sense of involvement on Ford's part, a film which makes new and significant use of the same basic plot. The contrasts between the films are all the more interesting for being largely a matter of emphasis. *Two Rode Together* seems terse and brief by comparison with the epic sweep of *The Searchers* but in fact they differ by only ten minutes in length. In the grating exchanges between Ethan Edwards, his half-Indian companion Martin Pawley and "Captain Reverend" Clayton (one of Ford's oddest combinations of religious and military values) *The Searchers* conveys a sense of detailed discussion and complex examination of values, when in fact its script relies far less on talk than *Two Rode Together*, where much of the conversation reflects a Hawksian use of dialogue as weapon. The deep thinking of *The Searchers* is subliminal, carried on in the Ford language of gesture, visual metaphor and action which he uses for his most personal statements.

One need look no further than the first shots of both films to sense the dissimilarity between their approaches, though it is a paradox that the opening of *Two Rode Together*, with indolent marshal Guthrie McCabe (James Stewart) dozing on his porch, chair tilted back like Wyatt Earp's in *My Darling Clementine* and feet braced against the post exactly as Henry Fonda's had been, is a more familiar Fordian image than the studied beginning of *The Searchers*. But, on second viewing, Ford's slow track in on the silhouetted figure of a woman who stands in the cool, dark room and looks out into the blinding red of the desert beyond, and at the figure of the man who dismounts and walks wearily towards her, is precisely evocative of the film's mood. Here are all the issues that will control the story; the woman Martha (Dorothy Jordan) and Ethan, her brother-in-law, whose unspoken love for one another will drive him on a futile search to recover all that remains of her, the daughter kidnapped in an Indian raid that causes the mother's death; the relationship between Ethan, always a wanderer, always outside, and the security of home and family that he must reject; even the landscape—Monument Valley, its red earth and stone—and the visual style—centres of bright sun surrounded by darkness—dominate the film, and Ford ends it, as he began, on the same door, a woman saying goodbye and Ethan moving on yet again. While copying an entire scene from *My Darling Clementine* to open *Two Rode Together* seems like laziness on Ford's part, the employment of familiar visual elements in *The Searchers* is apt enough to disarm criticism.

Redolent of Ford at his best, the long passage in *The Searchers* in which Ethan is absorbed into the warmth of his brother's home is a classic. Emblems of ritual predominate, ranging from repeated use of his name ("Ethan?", "Is that you, Ethan?", "That's you uncle Ethan," "Welcome home, Ethan") to the medal he gives his niece Debbie, although his contempt for the decoration ("It don't amount to much") suggests the unease with which both sides view this encounter, as society always views its meeting with those independent figures who do not obey the agreed rules of community. Ethan's brother Aaron (Walter McCoy) clumsily emphasises the rift by asking for money to finance the traveller's stay, and Ethan, no less doubtful, hangs his sword on the wall and remarks "I don't believe in sur-renders. I've still got my sabre." The group is held together only by the influence of the central female character, Martha, the calmest, most confident figure in the film. Organising, quietly dominating, she is secretly the vessel of unexpressed emotions, some of which Ford beautifully conveys in the famous shot where, as Ward Bond's Clayton sips his coffee in the empty room, he glances through a door, sees Martha stroking with obvious love the army cloak of her brother-in-law and pointedly looks away, aware that he has glimpsed a mystery which must remain secret.

Annelle Hayes as Belle Aragon, the barkeep in *Two Rode Together*, has less charisma, and though showing a confidence similar to that of Martha in *The Searchers*, her perception and control of the tension between Guthrie McCabe and Richard Widmark's Jim Gary, who has come to ask the former's help in recovering some Indian captives, is less moving than comic, and edged with a Hawksian sense of sexual competition. McCabe's cynicism and rejection of community and military values are developed in some neat confrontations; the marshal appreciatively sipping his morning beer brought by a deferential servant, and his ejection of two gamblers with the mere mention of his name, the temptation of Gary's dry and dusty troop of cavalrymen with offers of "a nice, cold beer." Belle, equally cynical, shows a sharper version of Martha Edward's insight, summing up Gary at a glance as honest, dull, of little interest to her, and suggesting as much. ("I can tell when a man comes in the

THE SEARCHERS. *Above : John Wayne. Right : Jeffrey Hunter and Natalie Wood. Below : Burial scene with Ward Bond*

door if he likes blondes or brunettes, whisky or beer, plays blackjack or poker.'') With similar abrasive humour, Ford handles a sharply funny conversation between Gary and McCabe as the troop pauses by a river, McCabe explaining his relationship to Belle and the sole temptation of marriage to her, that of replacing his present rake-off of 10 per cent of the town's income with the 50 per cent he would get as Belle's husband, Gary envious but quietly scoring where he can (McCabe: ''Y'see, she wears this stiletto in her garter.'' Gary: ''I know.'' McCabe: ''But *how* could you . . . ?'') As a character, McCabe is no more sympathetic than Ethan, both being self-interested, careless of other's feelings, cautious of the emotional and family attachments that motivate the community, but with Ethan we are aware of an element of personal anguish and of sacrifice McCabe does not share.

Visual and thematic similarities between the films are common. A moment of ritual dedication begins the search in each case, in *The Searchers* indicated by the discovery of a sacrificed bull, old Mose (Hank Worden) doing a crazy Indian war-dance and Ethan, in a close-up rare for Ford's outdoor dramas, staring back towards the farm which he now knows to be the object of the Indians' attack, and in *Two Rode Together* by the arrival of Gary and McCabe in the camp were the captives' families wait; ''They've been expecting a Moses or a Messiah,'' Gary explains to McCabe, and one woman says ''I saw a light shining on his head, like a halo. He'll find my son.'' The long-distance love of Martin Pawley (Robert Wagner) and Laurie Jorgenson (Vera Miles) in *The Searchers* that threatens to break up the crusade is echoed by Gary's romance with Marty Purcell (Shirley Jones), which impairs their quest. In each case, an object charged with emotional significance identifies the Indian captive; in *The Searchers* Ethan's medal, in *Two Rode Together* a music box whose tune the kidnapped boy recognises as he is dragged

TWO RODE TOGETHER. Top left : Gary (Richard Widmark) and McCabe (James Stewart) discuss Belle Aragon. Top right : arriving at the camp. Bottom : Ford outlines a scene with James Stewart, Shirley Jones and Linda Cristal

to be hung. Both films have a brutal reminder that years of life in the Indian community will have made the captives more Indian than white, and the horror of this process, and of Indian life, is emphasised often, especially in *Two Rode Together* with the cringing, white-haired captive who does not want to go back since she regards herself, as Ethan regards the much changed Debbie, as dead. Henry Brandon plays the Indian chief in both films, though with different emphasis; Scar in *The Searchers* is an arrogant warrior, but in *Two Rode Together* he plays the half-breed Quannah Parker, a self-interested politician anxious to trade his captives for rifles in order to guarantee his position and attract to McCabe the enmity of Stone Calf (Woody Strode), his main opponent and, fortuitously for Parker, husband of the kidnapped Mexican Girl Elena (Linda Cristal) whom he rescues.

The *déjà vu* brought on by a viewing of *Two Rode Together* is heightened by the sense that some elusive element is missing from this film that is present in *The Searchers*, the dimension of unspoken meanings in which the latter is rich. Clayton's pointed looking away from Martha stroking the coat is one of the film's most moving examples of characterisation in gesture, conveying as it does the man's respect for the privacy he has invaded, while Bond's playing, the movement of his head and the way he sips his coffee, hint at the deeper values of respect for form and family that will cause him to keep the secret forever. No less intense is a later scene where Aaron Edwards, standing by his door and looking out into the bloody light of the sunset, a particularly precise and studied Ford studio effect, senses that something is about to happen. A few birds fly up from a clump of bushes, and Aaron takes up his gun. "Think I'll kill some sage hens before supper," he says quietly to Martha, the mood and timing of the remark and her noncommital reply conveying instantly the deception consciously entered into to hide their fears from the children. The pose leads to a tension released when the daughter enters the room, goes to light the lamp, is stopped angrily by her mother and realises with a muffled scream that Indians have surrounded the house.

Ethan's character, a complex mixture of warrior independence, racialist bigotry, sexual obsession with his dead sister-in-law and, by proxy, his kidnapped niece, political conservatism and respect for those who meet his high standards of endurance and professional toughness, is revealed almost entirely through gestures, some so concise that they remain in the mind long after lines of dialogue have faded. His characteristic way of tossing down bags of gold, to pay Aaron, and to bribe the Mexican who leads them to Scar's camp, suggests a cavalier contempt for money contrasting with Aaron's careful storage of the gold in a hollow chair, thus underlining the self-interest that, to Ford, justifies the latter's death in the Indian attack. The weapon as a sign of character is also explored. Ethan's rifle in its fringed buckskin case is carried always in his right hand, even while riding, and flourished with the same imperiousness Ringo used to halt the coach in *Stagecoach*, but its constant readiness and the skill with which he uses it to kill both buffaloes and Indians eventually betrays the essential weakness in his personality that leads him to adopt killing as a cure for all the forces that threaten his way of life. He employs it with gleeful efficiency to repulse an Indian attack, ignoring protests from his friends that the Indians, after being beaten off, deserve a truce to treat their wounded and bury the dead, and later is equally ruthless in shooting down a herd of buffalo for no more logical reason than that he will in this way deprive the Indians of meat. For him, the rifle is less weapon than crutch. His skill contrasts with the showy but basically innocent gestures of the young lieutenant (Pat Wayne) who, in the process of offering his services to Clayton at the climax, makes a series of formal passes with his sabre under the nose of the baffled ranger. The lieutenant, like most of the younger generation in *The Searchers*, represents the coming peace and urbanisation, an *entente* with the Indians and an end to the war. His skill is pure show, not backed up with an ability to kill, and as such is viewed with contempt by the oldsters, to whom killing is the only answer. The sabre scene is in interesting contrast to Ethan's cleaning of his knife after hunting down the four Indians who have raped and murdered the older of the kidnapped sisters. Speechless, he sits on the ground and rips the bloody knife again and again into the earth, cleaning it and, in a particularly disturbing way, shouting domination over his physical environment.

The lack of a subliminal element in *Two Rode Together*, reducing as it does our appreciation to one level of meaning, is almost totally responsible for its inferiority to *The Searchers*. Characteristic Ford themes which appear in both are used in the latter with a power and dramatic appropriateness, as well as a believability, that the second film does not share; contrast, for instance, the symbolic importance of weapons in *The Searchers* with the carelessness implicit in McCabe's use of rifles as trade goods in *Two Rode Together*. Ford's favoured conjunction of a dance and a fight is made the climax of *The Searchers*, both the re-establishment of Martin's right to Laurie, placed in doubt by his long absence, and an affectionate return to the rituals of community from which it seemed he might be lured by Ethan's independence. In *Two Rode Together*, however, similar elements, even to the insistence on the proper ritual for the fight, Martin being invited to spit over a log as a challenge, Gary to knock a chip off his opponent's shoulder, are given little emphasis. Martin's fight dramatises to Ethan that he is again alone, changes substantially the conflict between Ethan and Clayton by neutralising the tension caused by the former's sudden arrival in the middle of a wedding ceremony and brings an acknowledgement by the community that Martin, despite his mixed blood, has a place in it. Gary's, on the other hand, is a minor midnight run-in with two pugnacious brothers, a dramatic diversion to add impact to the attempt by Mrs. McCandless (Jeanette Nolan) to flee across the river after the mental image of her lost child.

Where *Two Rode Together* has a unique interest is in its exploration of an aspect of Fordian morality. The film is essentially about personal honesty, financial and moral, and the contrast between them, Ford coming down strongly in favour of moral integrity at the expense of capitalism. McCabe, who has few virtues aside from personal honesty, is lured into an unpleasant situation by his trust, and encouraged to fulfil that trust by the good example of one man (Gary) and the bad example of another (the crooked businessman Wringle). That in doing so he transgresses countless other moral rules is immaterial, since none of them are rules by which Ford sets any store. Just as he sees temperance as a farce and drunkeness as noble, so Ford sees honesty as a virtue and such matters as McCabe's murder of the man whose wife he has taken, the graft from which he earns his living, and his frankly commercial view of the hostage hunt as of minor interest only. Respect for agreements—moral honesty—is vital to Ford's philosophy, since deception entered into by common consent and adhered to against all odds is the basis of communal spirit, and thus of society. Ford uses the same justification for drunkeness. Inebriation in company, like the dance and the song a shared vice, is an affirmation of community and therefore acceptable, while lust, envy, sloth, gluttony affect the individual and in his films are assigned only to those people he designates as villains; licence in the affirmation of community life is, to him, no sin. Only the sins against community—lechery, capitalism, theft—are shown as evil. *Two Rode Together* ingeniously dramatises this in the character of Major Frazer (John McIntire) who cordially despises McCabe and his motives, dragoons him into the army when he refuses to co-operate in the search, publicly expresses his intention to dishonour any agreement he may have made with him, and yet remains throughout a sympathetic character, since his motives are impeccable and he is scrupulously honest. Even when he determines to repudiate his deal with McCabe it is for a moral reason, an unwillingness to bargain with human lives. If he had shown any but a gentlemanly interest in the rescued girl, suggested sloth by being untidy, been less than stern in his disciplining of the officers who scuffle over Elena's attendance at the ball, he would instantly have earned our disrespect, but no such immoral characteristics are allowed to intervene. The only genuine villain in the film is Wringle (Willis Bouchey), the opportunist businessman who tries to make a deal with McCabe to pass off any captive boy as his stepson and thus placate his wife. "You're like me," he says to McCabe "You make you own luck," a rejection of group effort that disgusts McCabe and makes Wringle an unsympathetic character on the level of the dishonest suttler in *Fort Apache* who deceives the cavalry commander or Amos Force in *The Last Hurrah*, who will not admit his objection to Skeffington is sectarian and snobbish. Ford's characters can connive at an honourable deception, like that in *They Were Expendable* which smooths the death of a friend, but, as in all Ford rituals, it is the sharing that is important. Gypo Nolan's sin in *The Informer* is his attempt to hide his betrayal, not the betrayal itself, which even the victim's mother forgives. Cameo Kirby has the love of his girl until he deceives her father, admittedly for the father's good. The result of this deception and those that follow his assumption of another's identity nearly destroy him.

12. The Oldest Hero: The Last Hurrah

Among his films on the destruction of communities, *The Last Hurrah* (1958) represents Ford's furthest excursion into the modern world, whose homogenous and unstructured society he plainly despises. In what is ostensibly the story of one man's fight to keep alive some of the civic virtues of an earlier age, a fight he is doomed to lose, Spencer Tracy plays Frank Skeffington, four times mayor of "A New England City" (intended to represent Boston) and now hoping for a fifth term despite resistance from the city's entrenched conservative majority led by newspaper publisher Amos Force (John Carradine) and banker Norman Cass (Basil Rathbone). After a bitter campaign in which Skeffington's shrewd but old-fashioned manipulation of his popularity in the Irish-Catholic community is answered by his opponent's lavish expenditure on advertising and TV time, the old man is defeated, and shortly after dies of a heart attack, the last symbol of the old community life now completely destroyed.

Long, episodic, like *They Were Expendable* more fabric than story, *The Last Hurrah* is dominated by Tracy's lively performance as Skeffington, the assertive son of an Irish immigrant family who, although he has alienated his religious and political enemies—The Cardinal (Donald Crisp), the Protestant Bishop (Basil Ruysdael), the bankers and businessmen who inhabit the ultra-conservative Plymouth Club, symbol of a parochialism even Ford finds extreme—still retains their grudging admiration. As the Bishop says after refusing to back the clique's beaming idiot of a candidate, "I prefer an engaging rogue to a complete fool." The useful device of Skeffington calling in his newsman nephew Adam Caulfield (Jeffrey Hunter) to observe the campaign, which he fears will be the last of its kind, allows Ford to interpolate long passages in which the mayor re-examines his background, the community that has sustained him through a long political career and the social values he now sees about to be crushed by the soulless automation of Twentieth century life. The sense of an era coming to an end is accentuated by the constant reference in Frank Nugent's script to the gap between Skeffington's generation and that which follows, Ford generally preferring to suggest, as in many other films, that the new men are feeble-minded and inept, existing only in parisitical relationship to older masters. The mayor's own son, Frank Junior (Arthur Walsh) is a brainless playboy, Norman Cass's aging yachtsman heir (O. Z. Whitehead) a lisping cretin, cleverly used against his father when Skeffington appoints him Fire Chief of the city and threatens to let him make a fool of himself in fireman's uniform and official sirened car unless his father agrees to provide finance for a slum clearance project. Significantly, it is this move which, though successful, goads Cass into backing the campaign against the mayor, and their candidate, a toothy young Catholic (Charles FitzSimmons) is likewise part of the generation which, Ford feels, will destroy everything the previous one created.

An exception to Ford's dislike of the young, Adam, whom the older man treats as his unofficial heir, comes to love and respect

From THE LAST HURRAH. Left : Skeffington (Spencer Tracy) places a flower beneath his wife's portrait. Top right : Spencer Tracy with Edward Brophy and James Gleason at the wake. Bottom right : Tracy and Jeffrey Hunter.

Skeffington, assists at his campaign while the natural son is out on the town, is by his side when he dies and, in a significant gesture, automatically continues the old man's ritual of replacing the flower always kept in a vase before the portrait of his dead wife. Adam becomes a sympathetic and sympathising figure, but his acceptance of the mayor's ideas is not total. He disagrees in many respects with his uncle, understands but does not condone the blatant manipulation of his constituents by the party machine, notwithstanding the explanations offered by campaign manager John Gorman (Pat O'Brien) that vote-getting and community service can be combined. An employee of Force, Skeffington's greatest rival, and son-in-law of the most rigid of his Catholic opponents, Adam is identified with the forces that will crush the mayor and his outdated beliefs as Flint in *She Wore a Yellow Ribbon* and the young lieutenant in *The Searchers,* despite their respect for the elders, carry in their philosophy the seeds of the ethic that will destroy them. This realisation makes doubly poignant the final shot of *The Last Hurrah* where, as the black-coated colleagues solemnly gather at the mayoral mansion to pay their respects, Adam, his wife and father-in-law leave the house, conscious of intruding on a sacred moment. The knights must mourn alone over the body of their childless king.

Reinforcing this friction between generations is the more dangerous conflict of ideologies. Although Ford builds up memorable pictures of the two sides, Skeffington's dedicated team of friends and advisers against the mummified opposition of Force, Cass and their associates at the Plymouth Club, it is not immediately apparent that the root cause of their antipathy is sectarian, the Socialist Catholicism of Skeffington's Irish constituents against entrenched Protestant money and reaction. Naturally Skeffington is shown as blithely oblivious of doctrinal or social distinctions; among the brogues of his staff can be heard the Jewish voice of Sam Weinberg (Ricardo Cortez) and the public school accents of Winslow (Carleton Young). On the other hand, the Protestants are mercilessly pilloried in Skeffington's sudden arrival at the Plymouth Club, of which he is decidedly not a member, and his interruption of the group at dinner in the Cotton Mather Room ("You're kidding!" he says incredulously to a steward, bursting in shortly afterwards with the announcement "Gentlemen, bad news. The redcoats are coming.") It is only at this dinner-table confrontation, with Skeffington's charges that "your kind" never liked "our kind" that the basically religious nature of the conflict is outlined.

Having established the corrupt nature of his adversaries, who oppose him not for moral reasons but on the grounds of ideology, and emphasising this by the revelation that the mayor's feud with Force began when Skeffington's grandmother, a maid in the Force mansion, was sacked by Amos's grandfather for stealing two bananas, and that Force is himself an ex-member of the Ku Klux Klan ("I don't know why he left, unless it was because he had to buy his own sheet"), Ford turns to an affectionate examination of the mayor's beginnings and nature, an excursion into community life, the warmth and humour of which Ford responds to with the film's most firmly directed sequences. Taking Adam to the slum where he was born, and pointing out that the Cardinal, Adam's papal knight father-in-law and the mayor himself were all born in the same tenement, Skeffington relates his life to the narrow historical matrix in which Ford chooses to work, recalling the ailing Ireland of *The Informer* and *The Quiet Man* that contributed its people to the now-vanished vitality of the American/Irish slum society of the 1890s. Ford shows the mayor drawn to a dead and forgotten past, and his contemplation of the dark and silent alleys of the tenement suggests a world from which its inhabitants have retreated, leaving only Skeffington as a last lonely watchman.

This attitude is reflected in the compaign sequences, which seem intentionally anachronistic, redolent of the Twenties when Tammany Hall politics of the sort Skeffington represents were common. A simplistic attitude to power dominates the mayor and his rough diamond assistants, the ballyhoo of the election and such set-pieces as the wake for skinflint Knocko Minahan, the centre-piece of the film's first half. From Jane Darwell's totem appearance as Delia Boylan sitting alone at the back of the parlour where the body is laid out, the wake is pure Ford, with the humour, the parade of characters, the vitality of crowd direction in which he has few equals. From the lonely kitchen scene where Skeffington presses a thousand dollars on the widow (Anna Lee) with the unlikely story that it is a belated bequest from his wife, the sequence takes fire as news goes around the district that the mayor has come to the wake of the unpopular Knocko, whom nobody mourns. Baskets of food from the hospital are carried in by helpful policemen, but similar supplies of liquor from the customs house rejected by Skeffington on the grounds that Knocko never allowed a drop in the house, moral considerations obliterating the rather more serious abuse of his mayoral privilege in diverting community property to a private event. A similar contradiction offends Adam, who condemns Gorman's carnival attitude to the event ("It's a sell-out," the campaign manager comments with satisfaction when a contingent of police arrives to pay its respects) and the way he takes advantage of the meeting to instruct the "ward heelers" who get out the vote on election day. Gorman justifies this corruption of Catholic ritual on the grounds that politics are a more cheerful subject for discussion than death, but one takes Adam's point that Skeffington's methods, however much motivated by humanitarian considerations, are morally ambiguous. That we sympathise with Adam in this accentuates the degree to which *The Last Hurrah* shows Ford calling into question his whole attitude to the community-serving hero.

The details of the campaign are drawn by Ford with a broadness and simplicity that is initially jarring, Skeffington's effort seeming to consist mainly of parades and street-corner speeches recorded with a flat lack of involvement, while the "modern" campaign of the opposition is equally unremarkable. For a film that ostensibly deals with television and its effect on politics, the detail is inexact, Ford preferring to avoid any actual television images and merely surround the screen with a "TV set" frame. The grainy immediacy of the true

TV image is never used, nor does the technique suggest TV's ability to capture the excitement of events like an election meeting. Even though Skeffington in an early conversation with Adam says he realises his style of campaigning is on the way out, he, like his aides who call "fresh" a TV team that arrives at campaign headquarters to film Skeffington's admission of defeat, is unambiguously contemptuous of those who use the medium. The sequence of his opponent's "at home" broadcast is played as broad comedy, the candidate proudly displaying a life-size portrait of the Cardinal on his wall and launching into a prepared statement interrupted by the incessant barking of a dog (reminiscent of the Nixon "Checkers" speech) and the appearance of a wife who reads from idiot boards throughout. If this was his form, one feels, how did he win? And how did Skeffington, so patently a superior politician and clearly seeing the threat of his opponents, contrive to lose?

The key is in Skeffington's reverence for the past, the dominant factor in his personality, understandable since he is the oldest character Ford ever chose as a hero. In Skeffington, Ford sees the essential emptiness of a life devoted to tradition, in which mere age is an assurance of value. The inflexibility of the Plymouth Club begins to find its reflection in the mayor's actions as the film progresses, implying that he is destroyed not, as in Edwin O'Conner's novel, by the combined power of technology and new techniques of persuasion, but by his own irrelevance to the society he leads. His lack of understanding, his manipulation of the community for what he conceives to be its own good is suggested in an early shot where the mayor, respecting a tradition he has established, receives suppliant voters in the luxurious foyer of the mayoral mansion, sun flooding in through the open door as he greets with heavy political hospitality his first client. The contrast between his poor background and this piece of stage management interrupts our admiration of Skeffington, Man of the People, and hints at a later rightful collapse.

Skeffington is not, like Lincoln or MacArthur, a charismatic figure embodying the virtues of his society, nor a hero who inspires the community in time of danger and goes to his death peaceful in the knowledge that it has been saved, but rather a last dinosaur left behind by history, a casualty of the dead areas between great movements in which Ford often chooses to place his stories of communities in decline. A devotion to the past characterises many of his actions, most notably his continuing relationship with his dead wife whose portrait on the staircase of his mansion assumes a strong symbolic significance. The ritual of replacing the flower in the vase before it, adopted on Skeffington's death by Adam, the mayor's silent "conversations" with the portrait—a shrug on his defeat, a moment of meditation before it each morning—contrasted with his son's ignorant race up the stairs past it, earning our instant dislike; these, and eventually Skeffington's collapse before it show how central the image is to his life and, by implication, how meaningless that life has become. The conclusion of *The Last Hurrah*, again involving the staircase and the portrait, is, unlike most other Ford films, singularly lacking in hope. Only Skeffington's colleagues remain to mourn in the enormous mansion, as obedient in death as they had been in life. Their slow filing up the stairs in the last shot resonates subtly with an earlier scene where, returning to their office from the Minahan funeral, they unconsciously imitate the mayor in throwing aside black coats and hats, and tossing into corners their white scarves and carnations, because in both cases the ritual of death is invoked, the first shot showing it cast aside on the return to life, but the second, in the funereal step of the black-coated men as they mount the staircase and the hieratic figure of Cuke Gillen (James Gleason) at the foot, a formal symbol of grief, suggesting, unlike the hopeful shot of men walking along the beach at the end of *They Were Expendable*, a journey not into immortality but eternal forgetfulness.

13. Age Shall Wither: The Man Who Shot Liberty Valance, Donovan's Reef

The Last Hurrah began a new stage in Ford's career, marked by a contemplative, undramatic but often moving re-examination of concepts that were implicit in his earlier work. *The Wings of Eagles* (1957) is the last of Ford's middle period films, and its vitality, humour and affectionate recollection of prewar days were to appear less and less in the late Fifties and Sixties. "Spig" Wead, the pioneer aviator who became a scriptwriter after an accident had crippled him, was one of Ford's oldest friends and collaborators, and the celebration of his life in *The Wings of Eagles*, with Ward Bond playing, in Ford's clothes and with his coaching, a film director based on himself, is among his most personal statements, expressing a nostalgic love of the knockabout service life of the Thirties with an affection only a man who had not participated in it could have felt. But the films that follow are increasingly marked by a turning away from jokes and fights, and from the triumphant affirmation of human strength and determination which John Wayne's Wead conveys. *The Searchers* and *Two Rode Together* are films of violence, destruction, broken communities and lonely men, as is *The Last Hurrah*, and for the subject of his episode in *How the West Was Won* (1962) Ford chose Shiloh, the most costly battle of the American Civil War. His remaining films deal for the most part with age, time, the struggle of aging men to find a final meaning in the life they have struggled to build and protect. By using the same actors who had starred in earlier films, Ford emphasised the continuity of these later productions with the rest of his work, as well as showing how his attitudes had matured over the years. The concept of age, and of time changing the meaning of events is central to his later work, many of the films dealing with unresolved conflicts brought forward to the present, just as the films themselves carry on the conflict of earlier works. *Donovan's Reef* is a continuation of *They Were Expendable, The Man*

John Wayne and Dan Dailey in WINGS OF EAGLES

Who Shot Liberty Valance of *Stagecoach, The Horse Soldiers* of *Fort Apache*, with the character of John Wayne providing in each case a potent link.

All these films show, as well as a change in Ford's archetypal characters, a turning from the interest in landscape that was so central to his classic outdoor dramas, though the change was often dictated by his complete absorption of background into the theme, as in the case of *Donovan's Reef*. For a different reason, in *The Man Who Shot Liberty Valance*, the desert, though often mentioned, is

163

not evoked and barely seen, except in brief shots at the beginning and end. "Everything's changed," Hallie Stoddard says on her return to Shinbone, and although Link Appleyard says "The desert's still the same," in fact it has been destroyed, as Hallie comments at the film's close, transformed into a garden and stripped of the moral significance it had in films like *Three Godfathers*. Even *Cheyenne Autumn* (1964), the last of Ford's films in Monument Valley, passes over the deep significance of the valley's accumulated meaning to audiences in favour of a personal and picturesque approach to the problems of the Indian community. In all these films of the Sixties, an affirmation of strength and power is replaced by intimations of mortality, nowhere more brutally expressed than in Ford's episode of the Cinerama epic *How the West Was Won*, an unglamorous picture of Shiloh and its aftermath, with George Peppard as a young soldier caught up in a conflict of appalling brutality. The conclusion of the battle is one of Ford's most evocative passages, reminiscent of Whitman's descriptions of lamp-lit hospitals and men dying in torment, the elements grimly specific; mass graves dug by lines of men, a bloody operating table sluiced down before the doctor, anaesthetised by whisky, deals with the next patient; Sherman and Grant dragged from the eminence of leadership to become vulnerable and helpless men.

Of all the later films, *The Man Who Shot Liberty Valance* (1962) and *Donovan's Reef* (1963) stand out as statements of more than usual interest. While it does not justify the extravagant claims made for it by some contemporary critics, *The Man Who Shot Liberty Valance* shows Ford dealing intelligently and sometimes movingly with the subjects of ideals and example, and combining them with a comment on the betrayal of early beliefs which time and changing circumstances can bring. If Ford were a cynic, one might consider it a cynical work, casting doubt on his convictions, mocking acts he once considered admirable, but it is more a film of self-examination, from which the Fordian philosophy emerges with some of its superficial features destroyed but the basic structure intact. Its spare, puritan style and dull photography are initially daunting, but on reflection these become another sign by Ford that he is here dealing with a subject of intellectual rather than emotional force, a private meditation at the end of a long life. One recalls Mulcahey in *They Were Expendable*; "I'm not going to make a speech. I've just got something to say."

The plot, complex for a Ford Western, suggests some of the conflicting themes with which Ford's last films deal. Ransom Stoddard (James Stewart), an important Senator, and his wife Hallie (Vera Miles) return to their old home town of Shinbone for the funeral of an unknown recluse named Tom Doniphon. Urged on by his editor, a young reporter extracts from Stoddard the story of the friendship between Stoddard and Doniphon (John Wayne) when one was a young lawyer and the other a rancher famous for his skill with a gun, and of how, in a final shoot-out with the town bandit Liberty Valance (Lee Marvin), Doniphon secretly shot Valance rather than have Stoddard betray his pacifist principles, even though, in the eyes of the town and of Hallie, with whom both were in love, it was the lawyer who got the glory, and thus the girl. Stoddard leaves town with Hallie, and Doniphon, unknown, lives out a lonely life and dies forgotten, except by a few remaining friends, themselves outcasts. *The Man Who Shot Liberty Valance* is an apt footnote to *Stagecoach*, showing in detail that civilisation, though inevitable, destroys everything honest and good in frontier life, including the reliance on a balance of force among equals and the concept of a simple community based on rightful subservience to greater power, one in which people have no need to read or write since they share a free and open response to each other and to their environment. Ford chooses to show civilisation not as a gradual process of pacification and refinement but as an invasion by a stronger force, with Stoddard as its general and the concept of literacy as its most powerful weapon.

"Education is the basis of law and order," says a significant slogan on the blackboard of the school Ranse Stoddard sets up in Shinbone.

He is a man of books in an illiterate society where ethics are founded on personal behaviour and agreed religious and moral principles. His books represent a threat to that structure and they, as well as his use of the ideas they contain, are objects of his enemies' greatest anger. When the coach on which Stoddard is travelling to Shinbone is held up, Liberty Valance furiously kicks the books around and then beats their owner insensible. Later, the sign he hangs out indicating he is available for consultation as a lawyer is shot to pieces by Valance and his men.

The civilising process is not represented as Ford usually represents favourable processes, by the personification of their virtues in one man, but by a simple description of the assault Stoddard makes on Shinbone's ethics with the aggressive use of his literacy. His school diverts people from their rightful duties—Doniphon drags his slave Pompey (Woody Strode) out of a lesson—and even from pleasurable pursuits like fishing. He impresses on his pupils a devotion to a higher, political reality that transcends their simple culture, stressing not the rightness of his new Republican ethic or its virtue, but rather the electoral power it will give them, a power which Stoddard, in his work as a reporter on the newspaper, his ability as a politician, exhibited at a meeting to elect representatives to attend statehood talks, and even in actions like teaching Hallie to read and encouraging her employees to become American citizens, is alone able to use. It is Doniphon and not Stoddard to whom Ford assigns all the indications of worth and virtue—courtliness, skill, courage, a devotion to community principles—and he whom Ford regards as the true hero of the film, but Stoddard is cleverer, using Doniphon's strength, as he uses the electoral strength of the town, to increase his influence.

Throughout the film, a contrast is drawn between Stoddard and Doniphon that resembles that between Wyatt Earp and Doc Holliday in *My Darling Clementine*, one the cool operator, the man of power, the other a romantic hero, sensitive and compassionate but doomed to be destroyed by the stronger figure. The two characters, actually different aspects of the same personality, typify Ford's view of the West and its metamorphosis, and betray the essential ambiguity of his attitude to the process of change, a confusion not apparent in his treatment of religious or military traditions, which are eternal and immutable. Ford knows the West cannot survive, but wishes that it could, and suggests that, in a sense, it does live on in the legends its great men create. But the legends are empty, since they provide no example to those who follow, unlike those of Lincoln that survived in the structures they helped to create. Doniphon has lived a meaningless life. As he lies dead in a crude pine box in a cluttered stable, his boots stolen by a thrifty undertaker, he is attended initially only by his old slave Pompey and the deposed sheriff Link Appleyard (Andy Devine), reminders, like the dusty and wheel-less coach also stored there, of the culture Stoddard's relentless law and order has destroyed, as Earp's need to destroy the Clantons leads to the death of Doc Holliday at the O.K. Corral. That both Holliday and Doniphon sacrifice themselves willingly, having volunteered to accept their roles, is less comforting than in *The Fugitive* and *They Were Expendable*, since in those films men died for the eternal truth of religious and military belief, with which they were in total agreement; Ford's western heroes, including Doniphon and Holliday but also the thieves of *Three Godfathers*, agree to destroy themselves to uphold a cause with which they feel little sympathy.

Ford stresses the consciousness these men have of their role often in *The Man Who Shot Liberty Valance*, suggesting in Doniphon's attitude to Stoddard's arrival in town that the man's significance is not lost on him. Throughout the film he refers to Stoddard as "Pilgrim," implying a lack of allegiance on the new man's part to the community that sustains Shinbone. Stoddard, essentially, has no honour in Western terms, but is accepted by Doniphon because, by the standards of the new civilization, he is an honourable man, even though it is an honour Doniphon finds both alien and dangerous. The difference between their ethics is summed up in Stoddard's rejection of the opportunity to shoot down Valance, the man who has beaten him up. "I don't want to kill him," he says. "I want to put him in jail." If he had said, "I want to strangle him with my bare hands," or "I want to make him feel what I felt," our attitude, and Doniphon's, would have been different, but Stoddard disdains mere revenge; he wants Valance to be controlled in terms of his own ethics, and this Doniphon respects. As with Major Frazer in *Two Rode Together*, we ought to dislike him but Ford, by carefully withholding indications of self-interest, prevents us. Stoddard's action in stopping a gunfight in Hallie's café by picking up Doniphon's steak which Valance, hoping to cause trouble, has tossed on the floor would be an act of weakness were it not backed up by a strong statement of Stoddard's principles ("Can't you think of any way to solve your problems except to kill each other?"). Although the men of the West realise that these new principles will destroy their familiar way of life, a respect for another's ethics, if sincerely held, makes them accept with resignation the end of their world.

The Man Who Shot Liberty Valance is a sparse and grey film, its despairing story set in a landscape from which all emotional meaning has been stripped. Only the cactus rose, hardiest of desert flowers, continues to bloom, suggesting that a frail significance survives from the life of its forgotten hero. By contrast, *Donovan's Reef* is lavish in its use of colour, flowers and humour, a lively comedy of the South Pacific with Wayne and Marvin again playing with the ensemble skill they showed in the earlier film. "Guns" Donovan (Wayne), "Boats" Gilhooley (Marvin) and Doc Dedham (Jack Warden), stranded on the island of Haleakaloa when their destroyer was sunk during the war, carried on a guerilla action against the Japanese until the war ended. By tradition, "Guns" and "Boats," both born on the same day, beat each other up annually on their birthdays, and as the film opens "Boats" is deserting ship off the island to swim ashore and complete the ritual. Dedham, who has had three children by a native girl he befriended during the war, remained on the island where he runs a hospital, but is absent when a telegram arrives announcing that Amelia (Elizabeth Allen), his daughter by a previous

Woody Strode, John Wayne, Vera Miles and James Stewart in a scene from THE MAN WHO SHOT LIBERTY VALANCE

marriage, now the haughty if attractive boss of the family shipping line, is on her way to establish whether her father is a fitting heir to the family fortune, knowing that if he can be proved "morally unfit" it will go to her. In the end, Dedham reveals all and says he doesn't want the money anyway, Donovan is united with Amelia and, perhaps most important, "Guns" and "Boats" have their fight. The film is often very funny, but it is part of the contradiction in Ford's later work that, as *The Man Who Shot Liberty Valance* appears to be in praise of law and order but is less than admiring, so *Donovan's Reef*, while appearing to be a celebration of hedonism, is actually a bitter condemnation, as well as a work of considered moral force.

It begins with one of Ford's cleverest pieces of comedy. Gilhooley is mopping the deck of a ship while an island slides by in the distance. In the foreground is the brawny back of a petty officer, who slaps a large blackjack on the palm of his hand, out of Gilhooley's sight. Peering at the island, Gilhooley suggests that it is Haleakaloa, where the captain promised him the ship would arrive in the summer. The other man agrees. It *is* Haleakaloa, and they are there—though the captain never said they would drop anchor at the island. Shaking his head ruefully, Gilhooley says "Boats Gilhooley shanghaied! Well, it's lucky I've got a sense of humour." He then rounds on the man, lays him out with a mop and, pausing only to salute the bridge and snap "Permission to leave the ship, sir?", dives overboard and swims to the island, where ecstatic natives welcome him with a massed chant of "Gilhooley!" as if he is a Polynesian deity. Meanwhile, Amelia Dedham, presiding over the board of directors under portraits of the firm's founders, one a pirate in eye-patch and bandanna, makes known her intention to sail for Haleakaloa, a decision agreed to by the six venerable directors, including one odd old lady who, peering at a nugget of cigar ash dropped on the polished table by attorney Edgar Buchanan, blows it away with a sudden noisy puff and continues to beam as before. Neither scene, one mocking Navy discipline, the other family ritual, is especially appropriate to Ford's work and after this initial warning contradictions continue to pile up.

In Dedham's absence, and with the apparent intention of hiding the doctor's "moral unsuitability" from his daughter, Donovan takes over the three half-caste children and passes them off as his own to Amelia, to whom he is attracted. Much of the subsequent action is based on the misunderstandings this deception brings about, complicated by the romance between Donovan and Amelia, and attempts by the governor, De Lage (Cesar Romero) to attract her by discrediting Donovan. The idea of an entire film based on a deception is alien to Ford, as is the assertive character of Amelia and the mocking quality of the religious element of the film, with Marcel Dalio as a comic *curé*, and a bizarre Christmas Eve service at which policeman Sergeant Menkowicz (Mike Mazurki) appears as The King of Polynesia in a tableau of the Nativity wearing a pareu and headpiece of palm leaves and carrying a bowl of fruit, the governor's Japanese aide (Jon Fong) as the King of Japan wearing a kimono, and Gilhooley as the King of the U.S.A. in a white robe and gold paper crown carrying a horn phonograph. Gilhooley's desertion is perhaps understandable since he has been deceived, and is drawn by the necessity to carry on the ritual of the annual fight, and the deception of Donovan acceptable because it is connived at by all on the island to help out a friend, but the morality, for Ford, is dubious. The Dedham family is broken up, at much emotional discomfort to the children, merely to make the doctor appear to conform to a code neither he nor the island subscribes to, while the ritual fight, like that in *What Price Glory?*, is difficult to justify as an affirmation of community feeling, since it is personal and private. When at last the doctor returns and himself goes along with the deception, it becomes clear that the island and its morality are not what they appear to be.

Ford's connotation of islands with isolation and despair is here used with particular appropriateness. Far from being contented and happy, the people of Haleakaloa remain there out of necessity or fear. Donovan has created a financial paradise, always a suggestion in Fordian ethics of corruption and deception, but he lacks the comfort of a family which Dedham has accumulated and which, combined with a sense of obligation to the people, is his motive for remaining. Donovan's instant adoption of the children is in retrospect less a gesture to help a friend as one to enjoy, however fleetingly, the comfort of a genuine sense of community. One begins to realise that his is not the only deception by which the islanders live; the governor, forever sending off memoranda in the hope of getting a transfer, actually relishes his comfort; the *curé*, lamenting the state of his church roof, regularly distributes money provided for its repair to the poor, thus keeping the leaky church as a useful source of funds; the Dedham children, though appearing to share the native religious beliefs, are actually devout Christians, and, in a memorably prissy speech, Lelani, in answer to Amelia's question "Do you believe in gods and goddesses?" says "I believe in one god as we all do, but I respect the beliefs and customs of our people." Amelia's mission to the island is deceptive since, while appearing to be on a friendly visit, she is spying on her father. Although she cultivates a *façade* of virginal weakness and disdain, she can swim and water-ski as well as Donovan, if not better, and is not above inviting his sexual attentions with a tight bathing suit and enjoying the results. Her surreptitious lacing of her father's tea with rum and the subsequent conversation in which she recalls that the Dedham Line, avoiding the suggestion that it traded in the spirit, referred to it as "West Indian Goods," stresses that, like the Plymouth Club of *The Last Hurrah*, the Dedhams subscribe to the more dishonest aspects of Boston conservatism.

The people of Haleakaloa, like islanders in all Ford's films, are, we realise, not in paradise but escaping from it, maintaining their peace of mind with an elaborate set of deceptions eeked out with selective imports from the outside world. Like the old South, it is an economy supported by slaves and tradition, with white masters living in supremacy over the simple natives who provide an audience and work force. Gilhooley, superficially the film's least admirable character, emerges as its most moral, instinctively understanding his role as Lord of Misrule. When Donovan asks why they fight, it is Gilhooley who, indicating the crowd of attentive Chinese and natives at the window grinning in expectation of the next round, says "The tradition, the legend, the crowd," recalling the cynical self-analysis of Driscoll in *The Long Voyage Home* and the discipline *motif* of *They Were Expendable*, films in which Ford explored some of the same issues.

Donovan's Reef, Ford's last important film, eclipses the later *Seven Women* which, although both assured and provocative in its analysis of contrasts between professed religious and social feeling and the more real convictions sometimes held by apparent outsiders, relates essentially in theme to Ford's late Thirties and Forties period of soul-searching and realignment of religious convictions. So central are the issues of *Donovan's Reef* to Ford's dilemma as an artist that it is difficult not to see it as his final testament, and its analysis of morality as the most profound summation of a pre-occupation that has dominated his films. Conventional categorisation is less and less appropriate to Ford as his career progresses in skill and authority, and his last films, in which he is most in command of his subjects and less concerned than ever with the superficialities of entertainment, transcend descriptions like "comedy" and "Western" to approach the heart of his essential interest, the relationship of men to each other, and to God.

John Wayne and Lee Marvin fight it out in DONOVAN'S REEF

JOHN FORD: Films as Director

1917 *The Tornado* (2 reels)
The Scrapper (2 reels)
The Soul Herder (3 reels)
Cheyenne's Pal (2 reels)
Straight Shooting (His first
feature; 5 reels)
The Secret Man
A Marked Man
Bucking Broadway

1918 *The Phantom Riders*
Wild Women
Thieves' Gold
The Scarlet Drop
Hell Bent
A Woman's Fool
Three Mounted Men

1919 *Roped*
The Fighting Brothers (2 reels)
A Fight For Love
By Indian Post (2 reels)
The Rustlers (2 reels)
Bare Fists
Gun Law (2 reels)
The Gun Packer (2 reels)
Riders of Vengeance
The Last Outlaw (2 reels)
The Outcasts of Poker Flat
The Ace of the Saddle
The Rider of the Law
A Gun Fightin' Gentleman
Marked Men

1920 *The Prince of Avenue A*
The Girl In No. 29
Hitchin' Posts
Just Pals

1921 *The Big Punch*
The Freeze Out

The Wallop
Desperate Trails
Action
Sure Fire
Jackie

1922 *Little Miss Smiles*
The Village Blacksmith

1923 *The Face on the Bar-room Floor*
Three Jumps Ahead
Cameo Kirby
North of Hudson Bay
Hoodman Blind

1924 *The Iron Horse*
Hearts of Oak

1925 *Lightnin'*
Kentucky Pride
The Fighting Heart
Thank You

1926 *The Shamrock Handicap*
The Blue Eagle
Three Bad Men

1927 *Upstream*

1928 *Mother Machree*
Four Sons
Hangman's House
Napoleon's Barber (3 reels)
Riley, the Cop

1929 *Strong Boy*
The Black Watch
Salute

1930 *Men without Women*
Born Reckless
Up the River

1931 *Seas Beneath*
The Brat
Arrowsmith

1932 *Air Mail*
Flesh

1933	*Pilgrimage*	1948	*Fort Apache*
	Doctor Bull		*Three Godfathers*
1934	*The Lost Patrol*	1949	*She Wore a Yellow Ribbon*
	The World Moves On	1950	*When Willie Comes Marching*
	Judge Priest		*Home*
1935	*The Whole Town's Talking*		*Wagon Master*
	The Informer		*Rio Grande*
	Steamboat round the Bend	1951	*This is Korea!* (5 reels—
1936	*The Prisoner of Shark Island*		documentary)
	Mary of Scotland	1952	*What Price Glory?*
	The Plough and the Stars		*The Quiet Man*
1937	*Wee Willie Winkie*	1953	*The Sun Shines Bright*
	The Hurricane		*Mogambo*
1938	*Four Men and a Prayer*	1955	*The Long Gray Line*
	Submarine Patrol		*Mister Roberts*
1939	*Stagecoach*	1956	*The Searchers*
	Young Mr. Lincoln	1957	*The Wings of Eagles*
	Drums along the Mohawk		*The Rising of the Moon*
1940	*The Grapes of Wrath*	1958	*The Last Hurrah*
	The Long Voyage Home	1959	*Gideon of Scotland Yard*
1941	*Tobacco Road*		*Korea* (3 reels—documentary)
	Sex Hygiene (3 reels—		*The Horse Soldiers*
	documentary)	1960	*Sergeant Rutledge*
	How Green Was My Valley	1961	*Two Rode Together*
1942	*The Battle of Midway* (2 reels—	1962	*The Man Who Shot Liberty*
	documentary)		*Valance*
	Torpedo Squadron (1 reel—		*How the West Was Won* (1
	documentary)		section of 3—*The Civil War*)
1943	*December 7th* (co. Gregg Toland,	1963	*Donovan's Reef*
	who probably shot most of the	1964	*Cheyenne Autumn*
	2 reel film)	1965	*Young Cassidy* (Ford became ill
	We Sail at Midnight (2 reels—		after a few days' shooting and
	documentary)		the remainder of the film was
1945	*They Were Expendable*		shot by Jack Cardiff)
1946	*My Darling Clementine*	1966	*Seven Women*
1947	*The Fugitive*		

Select Bibliography

Critical literature on John Ford is extensive; the following is a selection of some generally available texts, including essays and books referred to in this book. Readers with a wish to pursue further Ford criticism should obtain a copy of the National Film Archive Book Library bibliography of Ford literature, to which I am indebted for many of the titles below.

BOOKS

John Ford. Peter Bogdanovich. Studio Vista, London. 1967.
John Ford. Philippe Haudiquet. Editions Seghers, Paris, 1966.
John Ford. Jean Mitry. Editions Universitaires, 1954.

SCRIPTS

Twenty Best Film Plays. Dudley Nichols and John Gassner (editors). Contains scripts of *The Grapes of Wrath, How Green Was My Valley* and *Stagecoach. L' Avant Scène du Cinéma* No. 22, 1963. *Stagecoach* (in French) *L'Avant Scène du Cinéma* No. 45, 1965. *The Informer* (in French) *Stagecoach* (in English), Lorrimer, London, 1971. *Theatre Arts,* August 1951. *The Informer.*

MAGAZINES—SPECIAL ISSUES

Focus on Film 6, 1971.
Présence du Cinéma 21, 1965.

MAGAZINE ARTICLES

Sequence 2, 1947. *John Ford* by Peter Ericsson.—11, 1950.
They Were Expendable and John Ford by Lindsay Anderson—12, 1950. *The Director's Cinema?* by Lindsay Anderson.—14. *The Quiet Man* by Lindsay Anderson.